Reviews of
The Six Stages of Cultural Mastery

"For us to become truly liberating leaders, we must learn to lead people of diverse cultures in a relevant way. *The Six Stages of Cultural Mastery* will prepare you to lead those unlike yourself with much higher levels of influence and power. You will want to buy several copies to give to others wanting to connect."

— Jeremie Kubicek, author of *5 Gears*, CEO and co-founder of GIANT Worldwide, named by Inc.com as a top 100 leadership speaker.

"Every leader serious about creating follower-ship and engaging talent of diverse cultures should read *The Six Stages of Cultural Mastery*. In an honest and refreshing way, Ricardo lays out very specific and actionable steps that will transform you, and through you, those you lead."

— Arnold Dhanesar, Group Chief Talent Officer, Zurich Insurance Company.

"We live in a fast-paced, hard-hitting world. *The Six Stages of Cultural Mastery* will help you to dig deep and do the necessary internal work to succeed with people of diverse backgrounds. Written with wit and wisdom, this book is a home run!"

— Molly Fletcher, author of *Fearless at Work* and *A Winners Guide to Negotiating*, CEO of The Molly Fletcher Company.

"Collaboration requires a deep level of self-awareness and understanding from a number of cultural perspectives. *The Six Stages of Cultural Mastery* provides leaders with a necessary framework for breaking down cultural barriers. It's a much-needed piece of the collaborative puzzle in a global economy."

— Alan Schaeffer, founder and CEO, Banding People Together.

"To work through the complex landscape of cultural diversity, one needs the right tools of engagement. *The Six Stages of Cultural Mastery* is a tool I highly recommend for your toolbox. Ricardo lays out a clear path to being a highly successful leader in today's culturally demanding organizations. This book will ready you to plug in and power up to lead and serve more effectively in any diverse corporate environment."

— Sharon Frame, author of *Wired to Win*, former CNN anchor and CEO of LeadHerShip.

"*The Six Stages of Cultural Mastery* will equip you to more effectively lead, sell to, and enjoy deep and long-lasting relationships with people of diverse backgrounds. Ricardo does a masterful job of laying out the specific stages leaders must follow in order to develop into Cultural Masters. ¡Bravo!"

— Pegine Echevarría, MSW, CSP, Member C-Suite Advisors, Motivational Speakers Hall of Fame Inductee, CEO of Team-Pegine, Inc.

"Leaders in today's world need to make sure that their voice is being heard clearly by people of all cultures and backgrounds. Ricardo has done a great service to all leaders to help them to find a voice that will resonate with others in a culturally relevant manner. This book will surely help you extend your influence in our world."

— Steve Cockram, author of *5 Voices*, co-founder of GIANT Worldwide.

"*The Six Stages of Cultural Mastery* takes leaders through a very refined process to move us to true levels of Endearment in Stage Six. This book should be read and digested by all organizational and community leaders as the insights Ricardo shares are transformational."

— Steve Akinboro, founder and CEO, LoveIQ and Council Member of the Gerson Lehrman Group

THE SIX STAGES

of CULTURAL MASTERY

A Roadmap for Leaders in a
Culturally Complex World

RICARDO GONZÁLEZ

Published by Bilingual America
In partnership with Leadercast Press
702 Old Peachtree Rd NW, Suwanee, GA 30024, USA
bilingualamerica.com

Ordering Information:
Quantity sales. Special discounts are available on quantity purchases by corporations, associations, and others. For details, contact the "Special Sales Department" at the address above.

First Edition

Ebook: ISBN-13:978-0-9988442-0-6
Paperback: ISBN-13:978-0-9988442-1-3
Casebound: ISBN-13:978-0-9988442-2-0

Contents

Acknowledgments

Thank you to my developmental editor, Patricia Heinicke Jr., for her amazing ability to keep me on track and for her marvelous suggestions to make this a better book.

My copyeditor, Mark Rhynsburger, deserves special credit for his gifts with language and grammar.

Book designer Joel Friedlander is a very cool guy who does great design and layout. Thanks for managing the pre- and postproduction of the book with such flawless expertise.

To Ginger Schlanger, thank you for your encouragement and for doing the very first edit on this content. You made me a better writer.

To my wife, Maribel, without you this simply wouldn't be possible. You are so amazingly patient and self-sacrificing. I love you!

Foreword

AS AN AUTHOR, SPEAKER, and business leader, most of my days are spent communicating—and candidly, up to this point in my life, I thought I was fairly good at it. But my skills fall woefully short of characterizing the life-changing thoughts and methodology that Ricardo González presents in *The Six Stages of Cultural Mastery*.

I truly believe that to match the power and potential impact of this book on the world, the foreword should have been written by the likes of Mahatma Gandhi, Nelson Mandela, or the blessed Mother Teresa. The positive legacy of those leaders is consistent with the lessons in this book—and the benefit that its readers could have on their family, community, organization, or nation is boundless. Every decade or so a book is written that can truly change the world. This is one of those books.

In our literature, there have been very few simple, digestible, and inclusive books that have the ability to create peace and harmony, regardless of the age, gender, religion, or political affiliation of the reader. Certainly, there are religions with their sacred writings, nations with their constitutions, and institutions like marriage, with their rituals and vows. But the simple truth is, many of those examples are *exclusive*. What Ricardo shares in these pages is *inclusive*, and I have no doubt that it could influence all of humanity.

I have spent my life studying people and serving others, and I have been blessed to call Ricardo a friend for a long time. Anyone who knows us knows that we've been living the lessons he shares in this book, and we have been fortunate to see the results firsthand.

I travel the globe regularly, working with dozens of diverse cultures. I promise you, if you follow the stages in this book, and remain open to the idea that to master culture, you must first master yourself—you can make magic happen with others.

Now it's up to you. If you've been wondering how to change the culture of your workplace, or are hoping to unite a community, or are taking on a bigger challenge like ridding the world of poverty, war, or hatred—this book is the answer. My hope is that you'll read, digest, and apply the Six Stages of Cultural Mastery, and that you will join us as we continue striving to make a positive impact on the world.

Humbly,
Duane Cummings
Founder, The Sensational Group; Former CEO, Leadercast

Preface

I GREW UP IN A crazy, bilingual, bicultural world where one grandmother was talkin' at me in her Southern drawl, "Now, Ricky, now stop that, Ricky! I'm a tellin' ya, Ricky, stop it now!" and my other grandmother was looking at me a bit more lovingly and saying, "Ricardito, por favor, mi amorcito lindo, ay pero Ricardito, ven acá a tu abuelita." You see, my father is Puerto Rican. He was one of 27 children and came to the United States with an eighth-grade education, speaking no English. And my mother was from the hills of Kentucky. So I am literally a Puerto Rican hillbilly!

My formative and teen years were painful as I watched two people from two very different cultures somehow try to make a go of it. Well, they didn't, and I suppose perhaps they couldn't. The culture clash in our family was quite dysfunctional.

So my interest in culture and cultural mastery is very personal. Every time I can help someone, or some organization, or some community get it right, it is redemptive to me. I experienced this many times in my work at Bilingual America, where since 1992 our mission has been to "bridge the gap between Latinos and non-Latinos so they can enjoy highly successful and productive business and personal relationships with one another" through cultural leadership and language training.

But over the years I noticed that even in this context, which by nature encouraged openness, people continued to stumble over cultural nuances. Why? What was missing?

Part of the problem, I realized, was that the thinking at the time (as now) was focused on diversity. And diversity is all about inclusion, tolerance, and acceptance. That's fine, but personally, I have never seen people work well together who are just tolerating one another, or just accepting of one another's differences. That's merely a baseline so we don't hurt one another; it's not necessarily healthy.

What's more, sometimes the push for inclusion and acceptance seems foreboding to people: It forces them to accept what they aren't prepared to accept based on their worldviews. When people are pushed to something they aren't capable of accepting, the obvious happens—they push back. This pushback creates cultural instability, strong judgment from both sides, divisions, and in the worst-case scenario, hate. Sound familiar?

Then, a few years back, the answer came to me.

I was on a flight to a conference, thinking it over, making notes on a napkin when it came flowing out—the Six Stages you're about to enter today. I felt excited and hopeful. The plane landed, I went about my business, I let the idea go. When I came back to it several weeks later it still seemed right. It still resonated.

We tested the Stages with clients for a few years, and I can tell you that the results are nothing short of life-changing. We have seen the Six Stages of Cultural Mastery fundamentally change how leaders work and engage with people of other cultures. In fact, I would go so far as to say that no business leader, public servant, or even diversity or multicultural manager can ignore these principles and enjoy the highest levels of success.

I'm very excited to greet you, and I expect great things from you. The world desperately needs Cultural Masters. We need *you*. Let's get it right.

—Ricardo González

Introduction: Why the Six Stages?

W E LIVE IN A time of rapid change in a very culturally complex world. Change creates cultural shifts. Rapid change creates seismic cultural shifts that can unsettle companies, communities, and countries unless people are properly led and managed. Corporate and community leaders in today's world must skillfully navigate rapid cultural shifts or get buried beneath the debris.

One of the countless recent changes that you've probably noticed is a shift in awareness about culture and diversity. We now have change management specialists, multicultural leaders, and even Chief Diversity and Inclusion Officers. Such titles or positions rarely existed less than 20 years ago. In fact, in 2005 less than 20 percent of Fortune 500 companies had a Chief Diversity Officer. These positions have developed rapidly over the past several years due to a combination of internal consciousness and external societal pressures.

The change has affected the structure of business and civic groups in other ways as well. Wherever we work, worship, and find involvement, Americans are holding trainings and seminars to try to achieve harmony. We hold seminars almost daily on bias—implicit, explicit, conscious, and unconscious. Due to an event in a single store unit, Starbucks decided to close eight thousand stores in the United States so that all store employees could undergo anti-bias training. FBI Director Christopher Wray recently assured lawmakers that agents will be required to go through anti-bias training. Due to heightened sensitivities, book publishers are even employing "sensitivity editors" to ensure that what they publish does not offend readers or arouse their negativity.

It's hard to know what effect all this is having. It seems we measure our success by the number of separate groups there are: We now have Hispanic groups, African-American groups, groups for women, Asian groups, LGBT+ groups, and more—all meeting in separate convocations with their own budgets and agendas. We have minority empowerment groups, ERGs (Employee Resource Groups, defined by ethnicity), Hispanic chambers of commerce, African-American chambers, Asian chambers.

It looks like a lot of activity, doesn't it? Yet we continue to struggle and stumble, perhaps more than ever. Negative biases don't easily go away, and instead of achieving harmony, we find ourselves farther away from one another. We continue to fight and tug and pull on one another's racial, ethnic, and cultural sensitivities. Nothing seems to have changed; if anything, things appear to be getting worse.

Although we have all this cultural movement and increased awareness, we still lack Cultural Masters—leaders who can inspire their people to the highest levels of personal and professional success, no matter their ethnic backgrounds.

Although we have all this cultural movement and increased awareness, we still lack Cultural Masters—leaders who can inspire their people to the highest levels of personal and professional success, no matter their ethnic backgrounds.

I believe that you can be one of these much-needed masters of culture, and that this book will help you along that path. The Six Stages of Cultural Mastery have the power to fundamentally transform you as a leader—and through you, those you influence.

A Frustrating and Disturbing Pattern

Several years ago, my staff and I noticed a disturbing pattern among leaders who went through our Success with Hispanics cultural leadership training at Bilingual America. This training teaches participants all about Hispanic culture and helps them to develop a strategic plan for how to successfully work with and do business with Latinos. But we noticed that after the training, back in the "real world," many of our clients continued to misfire. They would say or do things that were misunderstood, things that sometimes were actually quite offensive.

How could people who were well trained, people who could even pass a test on cultural competency, continue to do and say things that just didn't work, bringing consternation to all engaged? I was frustrated, to say the least.

Then I had an epiphany. I was on a video training call with a group of leaders from a company in Dallas, and I had just made a specific suggestion regarding a strategic approach to employee attraction. They laughed at me. They told me that what I was saying would never work, even though I knew it would, based on years of experience. At first, their laughter annoyed me. Then it made me think. What was the disconnect? These were smart people. How could they be so closed-minded? What weren't they getting?

Then I realized that I was putting the problem all on them, so I started asking myself better questions. What wasn't I giving them that they needed? What wasn't I teaching them that they needed to be successful in their cultural leadership?

These leaders were products of their own culture and experience, just as I was. Maybe they just weren't ready to receive the message. Maybe I needed to help them do the necessary *internal* work before they could effectively apply the *external* principles.

It was then that I started asking myself how one would, in fact, become a cultural master, or if you will, a highly skilled leader who knows how to lead people of diverse cultures. What does it take to become highly skilled in leading people of diverse cultures? This book is the answer to that question.

The Six Stages of Cultural Mastery give you the keys to unlock a big door—the door that many leaders hit their heads against as they attempt to manage and lead people from various cultures. If we follow and honestly work through these stages, both we and the people we lead will be transformed for good—and forever.

The Leader's Greatest Challenge

The greatest challenge facing today's leader is the challenge of leading diverse groups of people. Your organization has perhaps had trainings on "How to Avoid Cross-Cultural Faux Pas," "Implicit and Explicit Bias," "Cultural Competency in Corporate America," or even "How to Communicate with Your Millennial Workforce." But these can fall short, as you may have noticed. Because becoming a cultural master takes more than learning a few things about the people you work with and getting a few strategies for how to reach them, or not offend them. It certainly implies more than being culturally competent. I don't want to simply be competent and get by—I want to be a master and enjoy great levels of success in my cultural leadership. Without undergoing the deeper work, most of us will still likely find ourselves faltering in culturally complex relationships. At the very least, we won't come close to approaching the levels of success that is actually possible.

I've seen far too many leaders try to succeed with people of diverse backgrounds, only to fail—alienating or offending them at the most critical moments. In today's culturally sensitive environment, this type of failure can cost you your reputation, your career, and even your business.

My friend Arnold Dhanesar, whom you'll meet later in the book, took a cultural mastery trip with me not long ago. At the time, Arnold was Group Director of Talent and Development for the Americas at The Coca-Cola Company. Among our many great conversations during this time was one about today's new leader.

We discussed how early leadership teachings propagated the idea that IQ (intelligence quotient) was a differentiator. Leaders needed to have at least an acceptable IQ to have the credibility to lead. Then in the 90s the concept of EQ (emotional quotient) began to garner serious attention in the leadership community.

Now, in today's world, high CQ (cultural quotient) is an absolute necessity as businesses expand internationally and also hire large numbers of diverse talent. Arnold said to me, "Ricardo, the equation for today's holistic leader is truly IQ+EQ+CQ = The Super-Successful Leader."

The good news is that leaders can greatly improve their CQ. They can become Cultural Masters and succeed at the highest levels with their teams. The Six Stages of Cultural Mastery will provide you with a clear roadmap for how to lead effectively in our culturally complex world. The Six Stages will prepare you internally to enjoy high levels of success with people of all backgrounds and cultures. They will also protect you from making those unintentional, but serious, mistakes with people of other cultures. I can promise you that the result for you and those you influence will be life-changing. In addition, once you are a true cultural master, you will be in a much better position to lead meaningful cultural transformation in your organization or community.

These Six Stages will take some work. They will take commitment on your part. They won't come to you overnight. You will be tempted to skip some of the early stages but will realize that they truly do build on each other. Each stage is a building block, needed to reach the next one. The benefit, however, of being a cultural master is that you will reach a realm of leadership that few leaders enjoy, or perhaps even understand. Cultural mastery will separate you from the pack and allow you to effectively lead varied and diverse teams to much higher levels of creativity, productivity, and yes, profitability.

> *Cultural mastery will separate you from the pack and allow you to effectively lead varied and diverse teams to much higher levels of creativity, productivity, and yes, profitability.*

This isn't a long book. It's not a painstaking dissertation on culture. Think of it as a practical guidebook for leaders who sincerely want to become Cultural Masters so they can make a much greater impact on their organizations and their society.

The book's organization is straightforward: After a chapter defining and discussing culture, each chapter focuses on one of the six stages. In each chapter, I'll tell a few stories that illustrate the particular stage, and then share with you the meaning of the stage, the real barriers to its application, and exactly what you should do to develop in that stage. Some of the stories in this book draw from my personal and professional experience in the Latino[1] world, but this book isn't focused on Latinos. The stories simply serve as windows to a much larger world as you work with people of diverse cultures and backgrounds.

---

1   Technically speaking, the term *Hispanic* refers to people who speak Spanish. So it includes people from Spain, but not people from Brazil. Practically speaking, though, Spanish-speaking people outside the United States do not call themselves "Hispanic." They refer to themselves by their country of origin or as "Latinos." The term *Latino* refers to people from Latin America—Spaniards are Europeans, not Latin Americans. The fact is, most Latinos in the United States, myself included, use the terms interchangeably, although I prefer *Latino*. Many Latinos over 40 do not like the term Hispanic, which they see as derogatory.

The Six Stages Unveiled

Each of these Six Stages builds on the previous stage. At first, they may seem simple (as all truth is simple at its core), but they are not easily attained. They will stretch you, they will challenge you, and best of all, they will change you.

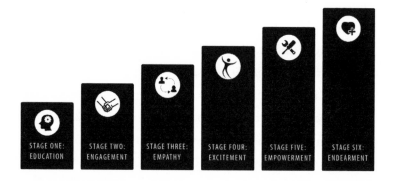

You will notice something wonderful about the Six Stages: They are balanced between emotion and action. Cultural leadership is not just *what you do*, it flows out of *who you are*.

Education, Engagement, and Empowerment all require you to act in a proactive manner. You must *do* something.

Empathy, Excitement, and Endearment are emotional in nature. They are all about the heart. If I don't do the internal, emotive work of these three stages, I will never truly succeed as a cultural leader. One word of caution here before we get started. Almost all leaders want to jump immediately to Stage Four, which is the vision-setting stage. It's tempting to completely skip Stages One to Three because we want to do something. But Cultural Masters are strategic. They understand that the stages of Education, Engagement, and Empathy are needed to create vision together.

Cultural Mastery is a skill set. It's not about being culturally sensitive—it is about being culturally skilled. This is a process for building deep and meaningful relationships with people culturally different from ourselves. Cultural Masters have the ability to successfully and consistently connect, create, and collaborate with people different from themselves.

Cultural Masters have the ability to successfully and consistently connect, create, and collaborate with people different from themselves.

In Stages One and Two we learn how to connect; in Stages Three and Four we learn how to create together; and in Stages Five and Six we learn to collaborate with one another for the common good. Each stage moves us naturally to the next stage.

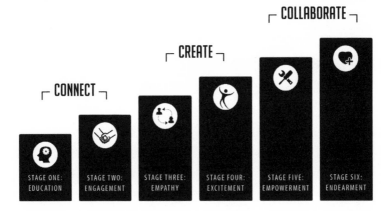

COLLABORATE

CREATE

CONNECT

STAGE ONE: EDUCATION
STAGE TWO: ENGAGEMENT
STAGE THREE: EMPATHY
STAGE FOUR: EXCITEMENT
STAGE FIVE: EMPOWERMENT
STAGE SIX: ENDEARMENT

Before we get started on the Six Stages of Cultural Mastery, let's discover together what culture really is and how it works.

What Is Culture?

THERE IS NO WAY for us to become Cultural Masters without an understanding of what culture is and how it works. This chapter will set an important foundation for our considerations throughout this book. It forms the backdrop against which all Six Stages will play out.

Culture, simply put, is the DNA of a group, organization, or society. It's the product and the expression of a people's shared experience. It both defines and drives the group. It defines the internal relationships of the group, and it drives the behavior of the group members both internally and externally. Yet it's not static; it's constantly changing.

Culture *is*. We must understand this before we go any further. Culture *is*. (As Immanuel Kant, the eighteenth-century German philosopher, said, "What is, is.") In other words, a culture, in itself, is neither right nor wrong. It simply is.

Certainly, every culture has elements that work and elements that don't work. We are all human—we all do wrong and our wrongs can be perpetuated in our cultures. But once I start judging another culture, I judge the people of that culture. Once I judge those people, I disqualify myself from leading or working with them. This does not mean that I don't believe in good and evil or right and wrong. I simply don't

Culture is. Culture is learned. Culture is transmitted. Culture permeates. Culture drives. Culture defines. We are all shaped by our cultures.

believe one should be so arrogant as to say that one culture is *better* than another, or to behave as if it is.

We may not like some element of a culture, we may not agree with it, we may even think it's wrong, but that judgment won't change anything for the better. Culture is, and until we accept the realities of a given culture without making moral judgments on it or its people, we have no chance of working effectively within its constructs. If we do not fully accept the realities of a given culture, we will be frustrated as leaders, and we'll also be frustrating to those we lead from within those cultures. Whenever we make judgments on another culture, we take ourselves out of position to actually have positive influence in and on that culture. *We simply cannot lead people effectively if we are resisting them or their culture emotionally.*

We'll learn how to avoid this resistance throughout the book. First, let's look at the sorts of things you can find in every culture.

The Main Elements of Every Culture

To understand a given culture, one way to start is to look at its parts. The following five elements are present in every culture, whether it's a community culture, a corporate culture, or even a family culture.

1. Beliefs

Cultures rally around common core beliefs. This is why organizations rally around mission or vision statements. This is why religions all have stories that illustrate their belief systems. And why movements publish manifestos. And countries have constitutions. Typically, when people come together as a group, they do so around a common set of expressed beliefs.

2. Values

These are the foundational aspects that a culture deems good or valuable. Values grow out of a culture's belief system. For example, some cultures value individualism and see it as a good and desirable thing. This value may be based, in part, on a belief that the group does better when individual talent and skill is fostered and supported. In other cultures, a person's contribution to the group is much more important and rewarded than individual achievement, and this value may be based on a belief that the whole does better when everyone knows where they fit in. Values have a significant impact on how people within a culture behave and develop.

3. Language

Every culture has its own language. This may be an actual language, such as English, Spanish, or Arabic, or it may be the "lingo" that is spoken within a particular culture. Religious groups, for example, have their own language. Every culture's youth has its own lingo. Language is necessary to effectively communicate beliefs and values to the members of the culture.

4. Norms

Every culture has expectations of its members. These norms can be written (laws, policies, encyclicals) or unwritten. Norms outline expected behavior. Members who do not follow the norms may be seen as odd or rebellious. They may be ostracized, marginalized, ignored, or in the worst cases, separated from the group through firing, expulsion, imprisonment, or even death.

5. Symbols

Cultures have ways in which members identify and brand themselves so everyone knows who they are. Countries have flags and monuments; religions have flags and symbols; companies have brands and logotypes; teams wear a common uniform and have an identifying symbol on their hats, helmets or shirts (often worn by fans as well); gangs have identifying clothing or tattoos; families have a common last name. You can even look at food and dress and possessions like cars and homes as cultural symbols. These are the symbols that bind together a culture.

Of course, there are other elements, like religion, music, art, sports, health, government, and law, that are found in many cultures. But not *all* cultures. Your organization probably doesn't have a common religion, for example, or a traditional dance. (Although maybe it does, and you see it every year at the holiday party!) But in all cultures, including the one you lead, you can find these five elements.

What About Race?

You may notice that race is not listed here as an essential element of culture. That's because even defining race is difficult; it depends on the discipline that's defining it. Many of us are quick to accuse others of racism when the reality is we may be dealing more with ethnicism or culturalism.[2] What looks like racism is often something else.

---

2   According to Wiktionary.com, "ethnicism" is now used to mean "a prejudice based on ethnic origin."

For example, *Latino/Hispanic* is not a racial group. The group is, in fact, composed of people of all racial groups. The broad group we know as *Latino/Hispanic* is also composed of many nationalities: Puerto Ricans, Mexicans, Cubans, Colombians, Argentines, and so on—all with their own unique cultures. And within the national groups is a multiplicity and a blending of ethnicities. The common bond is the Spanish language, and of course, language is an essential element of culture. But even there, the closer you look, the more complex culture gets. For many people who might be identified as "Latino," the primary language is not Spanish but Nahuatl, Mixtec, or one of the many other languages indigenous to Central and South America.

This kind of nuance is also at work among peoples with African ancestry; African-Americans can be seen as an ethnic group distinct from, say, Jamaicans, or Senegalese, or Nigerians. In the traditional *Asian* racial category we have multiple ethnicities, including Japanese, Taiwanese, Korean, Chinese, and more. And within each of these major ethnicities, there are many subcultures.

So, we should be very careful about our use of the words "racism" or "racist." The reality of a particular bias or stereotype may be more rooted in ethnicism, or we might even say, culturalism. This is important because Cultural Masters do not use cultural terms loosely and are precise in their thinking and semantics.

The Iceberg Analogy and How Culture Shapes Us

A helpful way to look at the elements of culture is presented in "the Iceberg Analogy of Culture." This excellent analogy, developed by Edward T. Hall in 1976, essentially says that a culture, like an iceberg, is partly visible but mostly invisible.[3] The visible elements of culture are those at the tip of the iceberg—surface things that we can see, touch, hear, taste, and smell, like food, music, dress, religion, language, and behavior. The invisible, intangible elements of culture, the things we don't quickly see or understand, are deeper, more internal elements like beliefs, values, gender roles, social norms, concepts of time, and so on. Plus all the assumptions and prejudices that go along with these.

---

3   Edward T. Hall, *Beyond Culture* (Anchor Books, 1976).

What's above the water line in culture is pretty easy to identify—like special dishes, or a traditional song or religious ceremony. These items are learned explicitly. And they're relatively easy to change. When people come to a new country, for example, within a couple of generations they often let go of big chunks of their tip-of-the-iceberg culture—things like their traditional dress, their diet, even their language.

The under-the-water parts of culture are more unconscious, and therefore they change more slowly. They're not learned explicitly, as are a dance or a recipe, but through a kind of osmosis, or assimilation.

Take our beliefs about the value and meaning of work. Where did we get those beliefs? Our parents didn't sit us down and give us books to read on the subject. Instead, we learned what we believe about work by watching our parents and other people work; we learned without really knowing we were learning. As a consequence, we can find it hard to realize that there are other ways of looking at work.

In fact, it's usually not the external parts of culture that get us into trouble—it's the internal, intangible parts. We may have no problem when someone's clothing, music, or food is different from ours; we may really love that diversity. But watch out when our concept of work or time runs up against someone else's: Icebergs colliding!

Let's take a little journey together to see how all the elements of culture, tangible and intangible, pervasively influence us. For the reality is, we are all shaped by our cultures. And by that I mean the culture we grew up in, the culture we learned as kids.[4]

Take me, for example. I grew up in the Puerto Rican island culture in the 70s, and sure enough, I love eating rice and beans and fried plantains. I love the music of Hector Lavoe and El Gran Combo de Puerto Rico. My favorite game is dominos and I drink strong coffee, just like my *abuela* used to give me. These are some of the ways my culture has shaped me.

Then there's my friend Carlos, who grew up in Mexico, and sure enough, he roots for El Tri (the Mexican national soccer team), reveres the music of Vicente Fernández and Ana Gabriel, and instead of listening to the Red Hot Chili Peppers, he eats them! Carlos is Catholic, and he has a deep respect for the elderly. (He lives not only with his wife and kids but with both his mother and his mother-in-law!) These are some of the ways Mexican culture has shaped Carlos.

My friend Warren is white and grew up in the Deep South of the United States. He loves corn bread, grits, BBQ, and country music, and he attends church every Sunday—and most of the time even on Wednesday nights. Of course, there are some other things about him that one wouldn't automatically associate with Southern culture, but these are just some of the ways that culture has shaped him.

You get the point, right? Chances are, if you were born into an Amish farming community in Shipshewana, Indiana, and

---

4   As you think this through you may realize that you live in several cultures at once. There's a culture at work, and one at home. There's the culture of your faith. If your family is bicultural, then you straddle cultures there. There's your regional culture, your national culture, your corporate culture and so on. (The deeper we dig, the more varied and beautiful our world becomes.)

decided to stay there, you would wear plain Amish clothing, not use electricity in your home, farm your land with nonmotorized equipment, and if a neighbor's house burned down, you would help rebuild it without question.

Chances are, if you grew up African American in Harlem in the 80s, you would enjoy, or at least appreciate, hip-hop music. You would likely have voted for Barack Obama, and perhaps you'd believe that you have to work double hard to make it because the system is not stacked in your favor.

We could go on with other examples. Of course, individuals respond to culture in unique ways that don't fit our expectations. There are outliers in every society: Many Mexicans are not Catholic; many Southerners don't enjoy grits; many African Americans belong to the Republican Party. The point is—in most cases, our first culture, from its food to its politics, has an impact on our tastes, our activities, and our beliefs.

Can you imagine what your life would be like today if you had been raised in a different culture? It's difficult, isn't it? Trust me, it's hard for me too. We'll get there. But before we strain our brains too much trying to imagine that, take a moment and think about your own culture.

Ultimately, you'll want to understand and master the culture (or cultures) of the people you lead. But let's start with *your* culture, the culture of your family of origin. An important step in becoming a cultural master is learning to recognize the shape of your *own* cultural iceberg, the one you grew up on. That's the culture that really shaped your under-the-waterline beliefs and values. What are the tangible, external parts? The internal beliefs and values? Starting with the five elements of every culture outlined above, what did your family's culture look like when you were a child? What were its core beliefs? Its values? What language was spoken in your home? What were some of the social norms that dictated correct behavior? By what symbols did your family and neighbors express their identity?

Don't expect everything to be logical or consistent. Culture is rich and complex; it's an intricate mosaic—that's the beauty of culture. The more fluent we are with culture, the more comfortable we become.

You can use the image on the next page to begin to consider your own cultural iceberg:

Culture is. Culture is learned. Culture is transmitted. Culture permeates. Culture drives. Culture defines. We are all shaped by our cultures.

If we don't, or won't, accept that culture is the driving force behind virtually all human behavior, then we will never become Cultural Masters and will be rendered incapable of effectively leading people from multiple cultures and worldviews.

Now that we have a clearer understanding of culture and its impact, let's unveil Stage One of Cultural Mastery.

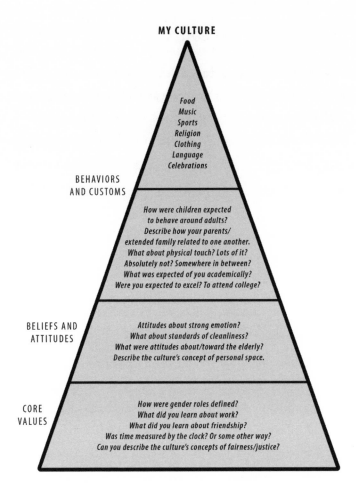

Resources

- **Iceberg analogy of culture:** Do an Internet search for this phrase and you'll find an endless supply of explanations and lessons. Hall's book *Beyond Culture* (Anchor Books, 1976) and his other works as well provide one place to start.

- **Culture:** Of course, your investigation of ideas about culture could last a lifetime. One fun way to initiate your search is to go to YouTube, watch a video, and let YouTube make more suggestions based on your choice. Same for other video sources such as Netflix and Amazon. Here are a couple of ideas for starters:

  - "India Is Not Chaotic." TEDx talk by Dr. Devdutt Pattanaik. youtube.com/watch?v=xKOh9DfQBgU

  - *What Makes That Black?* Books and website on the African-American Aesthetic. amzn.to/2mqcp34. I would also recommend watching Smokey Robinson's Def Jam Poetry titled "Black American" on YouTube. It will introduce you to a modern singer's view of being a black American as opposed to African American.

- **Google Alerts:** If you want to stay up on a particular culture, or cultural events, simply go to Google Alerts and ask to be kept updated. Every time something comes up with your keywords, Google Alert will send you an email with a link to that article or event. This is a great way to stay up on current events in the culture of your choice.

STAGE ONE

Education

*Education is the most powerful weapon
you can use to change the world.*

—NELSON MANDELA

"**W**HY ARE LATINOS SO gross?" "Why are Latinos so ungrateful?"

These questions came to me from two of my clients, non-Latino business leaders. Please don't judge them too quickly. They were not trying to be offensive—in fact, believe it or not, *they* were feeling offended by the Latinos they worked with!

Until I heard the first question, I had never thought about Latinos being any more gross than other people. I've learned not to react to people's questions about culture, realizing that everyone forms an opinion for a reason, so I just asked my client to explain what he meant.

He said that he had tried for some time to get his Latino workers to put the toilet paper into the toilet after going to the bathroom. But they just wouldn't do it: Even after he put up signs and spoke to them about it, they would still put the soiled toilet paper in the trash! Sometimes they would miss the trash can altogether and it would just land on the floor. To him, this was just disgusting, and he was at the end of it with these guys.

> I've learned not to react to people's questions about culture, realizing that everyone forms an opinion for a reason.

So I asked him a simple question: Had he ever traveled into poorer areas of Latin America. He had not. Then I asked him if he was aware that due to plumbing issues in those areas, many Latinos had been taught their entire lives *not* to put toilet paper into the toilet, but rather into the trash can. He said he hadn't been aware of this. Then I showed him pictures of signs from various Latin American countries, clearly telling people (in Spanish) not to put the toilet paper into the toilets.

Once he understood this, my client was able to stop resisting his people emotionally. Then he was in a position to shape a more effective solution for getting the toilet paper into the toilets.

The second question, "Why are Latinos so ungrateful?," was even more surprising because that idea was counterintuitive for me. I had always heard Americans talk about how loyal and hard-working their Latino associates were. I had never been approached with their supposed ingratitude before. So, I did what I normally do and simply asked for clarification.

My client explained to me that for Thanksgiving, his organization had given turkeys to the Mexican workers, most of whom were first-generation immigrants, but no one said so much as *gracias*. I remember looking at the guy and smiling.

He asked me what I found so amusing, to which I replied, "I've personally never seen people in Mexico eat turkey on Thanksgiving. Now, I'm not saying no Mexicans ever eat turkey, because that's not the case. It's just that Americans eat turkey on Thanksgiving due to an American tradition, and it may not be a gift that resonates much with these workers."

My point: Sometimes we judge another's behavior or attitude as negative because we simply don't understand where they are coming from. We don't know much, if anything, about the people we're working with or leading.

What's more, we all have a tendency to expand our negative judgments to include an entire group. This is how stereotypes are perpetuated. So a few workers dumping used toilet paper into a trash can become "gross Latinos." Some employees who are unresponsive to a gift become "ungrateful Latinos." It's not unusual—we do it all the time, mostly without noticing. But this kind of stereotyping limits our ability to see the whole person, to appreciate what's really going on. It weakens our leadership, and Stage One is key to avoiding it.

We simply cannot lead people effectively if we are resisting them or their culture emotionally.

Both of my clients, after hearing a likely explanation, were initially embarrassed and apologized for insulting their Latino associates, and Latino people as a whole. Both of them, to their credit, understood that they made these assumptions simply due to lack of knowledge. Nor did I see them as bad people, or people I should make a public spectacle of for "offending Latinos"—I've learned to avoid that kind of rush to judgment. And I know that we all have levels of ignorance (lack of knowledge) about a lot of things. Let's cut one another some slack and solve this for the common good. We need to move past wanting to hurt people because they say or do something out of ignorance. I prefer to gently help them see a better and more productive way.

Influencing Through Understanding

A few years ago, I was scheduled to speak at an association conference in Dallas, Texas. The executive director of the association pulled me aside a few minutes before my speech and pointed to a guy in the audience. "Ricardo," he said, "do you see that gentleman over there?" I nodded. He told me that this man was not happy that I was going to be presenting, since he was "a good ol' Southern boy set in his ways who doesn't really care much for Latinos." He warned me that I should be prepared for a challenge. I understand that everyone arrives at their point of view through their own cultural framework, so I assured the director that everything would be fine.

During my speech, sure enough, the gentleman did challenge me, more than a few times, and I was able to answer his questions in a respectful and honest manner. After the speech, I went up to him and thanked him for his interest (even though most people would have been tempted to call it his bigotry or prejudice), and we each went our own way.

One thing that I've learned in helping leaders transform their thinking is that if I push them, they are going to push back. In fact, the harder I push them, the harder they push back. If I humiliate them—well, then I've probably lost them forever. If, however, I validate them and acknowledge where they are coming from before trying to educate them and influence their thinking, many respond positively, and it makes an incredible difference in their lives and their relationships within their organizations. You see, our role as cultural leaders is not to call people out, it's to cuddle people in.

So what happened to the good ol' boy? Two years later, I was about to give a speech to a group of business people in Phoenix. As I was being introduced, a gentleman in the audience stood up and blurted out that he wanted to say something before I spoke. I looked more closely, and there was the same guy from the Dallas conference. I hadn't seen him in two years, and here he was again, unsettling the order! So I'm thinking, Uh oh, this guy's coming after me for sure.

> *Our role as cultural leaders is not to call people out, it's to cuddle people in.*

As God is my witness, when he was given the floor he started to cry. In his beautiful Southern drawl he said, "I just wanted to say to y'all to listen to him. I heard him talk a few years back and it changed my life. I learned to love them Latinos—those there are good people. My business is so much better and I'm a whole lot better man."

I was absolutely stunned. I could never have paid for an endorsement like that.

That gentleman, Thomas Sproul, died a few years ago, and he's in heaven with a whole lot of Latinos whom he actually loves. This is the beauty of becoming Cultural Masters. Not only do we become very skilled at something important, not only do we grow our organizations and our teams, but most important, we grow our hearts and become better human beings.

What Is Cultural Education?

Before we get into all kinds of advice on how we should educate ourselves regarding a particular culture, let's first find out what it actually means to be educated.

The word *educate* comes from the Latin word *educare,* which means "to bring up," "to train," or "to lead forth." Cultural education is a process. It is not a one-time event. Cultural Masters are forever learning.

That this is a lifelong learning process is especially important because cultural currents can shift and change quickly in the modern world, and true Cultural Masters stay ahead of these currents. Cultural education is simply a training of our minds to clearly understand where the cultural currents are moving while appreciating their historical wellsprings.

It's like being tech-savvy. What I learned about technology in the 1980s is completely obsolete today. However, an understanding of technology from those days may provide a basis for understanding how we got where we are today. And to stay ahead of the tech game, we need to constantly update our knowledge. Cultural education is like that.

> *Cultural education is simply a training of our minds to clearly understand where the cultural currents are moving while appreciating their historical wellsprings.*

To understand where we are today, we must also understand from whence we come.

Barriers to Cultural Education

If cultural education is a process of mental training, why are some of us finely attuned to cultural matters and others are not? Some of us have never educated ourselves about the cultures of those with whom we work or do business. Some of us actively resist any offers to help us learn. Why?

There are three barriers that can keep us from receiving the cultural education we need: bigotry, insecurity, and laziness.

1. Bigotry

Bigotry is intolerance of people who hold different opinions. Bigotry goes beyond the unintended stereotyping that we've all experienced in that it's a pervasive attitude of superiority: We are better than you. My way or the highway!

This is not a problem that we've left in the past with Archie Bunker. For example, the 2016 U.S. presidential election brought out a great amount of bigotry on both sides of the political spectrum. Civil discourse came to a halt for the most part. Intolerance for one another was at an all-time high. People lost friends left and right over their political viewpoints and candidates.

If we are bigoted in any way it is a clear barrier to our ability to honestly and openly learn about other cultures or points of view. Bigotry limits our leadership and hinders our influence. Now's the time to examine those areas of your life in which bigotry is lurking. Who do you feel superior to? Which group do you allow yourself to belittle, even in jest or only in your thoughts? Relax. We've all got those dark corners. Bring them out into the open, take a good look, and commit yourself to healing.

2. Insecurity

Let's face it—any challenge to our longstanding views can put us on the defensive. When my deep iceberg collides with someone else's, it can feel as if my core values are being shaken, even threatened. Examining our own views and learning about someone else's isn't for the faint of heart.

Is it emotionally tough for you to challenge your long-held viewpoints? If so, that's OK—you're not alone. Our pride tells us we are right about things. Our fear tells us not to entertain the idea that we might *not* be right. Just remember: You won't come close to reaching your maximum potential in a closed-off world. Stretch yourself and you'll find that you won't break—rather, you'll break *out*.

> *Our pride tells us we are right about things. Our fear tells us not to entertain the idea that we might not be right.*

3. Laziness

There's no other way to put it—some of us are just lazy learners. We want the benefits of learning without the hard work that learning sometimes requires.

Are you a lazy learner? Perhaps you're just innately smart and haven't had to work too hard at learning most things. Good for you. But culture can be incredibly complex, and becoming a cultural master will require some serious interaction on your part, no matter your level of intellect.

These three barriers have kept countless leaders from reaching their full potential and impact on those they lead. But I believe you can be bigger than the barriers. You can start simply by opening a book, watching a movie, going to an ethnic restaurant...

Seven Elements to Learn about a Culture

Remember that Stage One is a process. It requires action on our part. We have to set out a learning plan or path. So how should we educate ourselves about culture? What exactly should we learn?

The purpose of this section isn't to educate you about everything there is to know about a specific culture. That would take volumes, no matter the culture. My intent is to help you learn the general categories of things you need to understand about a culture. It will be your job to seek out the specific cultural education you need, depending on the group of people with whom you most need to engage.

Remember the iceberg you created in the previous chapter, "What Is Culture"? That was your personal cultural iceberg. Here in Stage One you'll be working on understanding another iceberg—that of the people you lead.

1. Language

Learn the culture's language. If you want to truly understand the Latino culture, for example, learn to speak Spanish, and speak it well. (By the way, there are more first-language Spanish speakers in the world than first-language English speakers.) If you want to work with Egyptians, learn Arabic. If you want to work with people from China, learn Mandarin or Cantonese. If I were going to master three languages in business, they would be English, Spanish, and Mandarin Chinese, in that order.

I have heard many business leaders say that they don't need to learn the native language of their associates because their associates speak English. Yes, they may speak English fluently. And you may be able to communicate with them at an acceptable level for business purposes. But unless you learn their native language, you'll never reach deep into their souls. And the reality is, *we cannot lead people to the highest levels until we know them at the deepest levels.*

Think about those times when your colleagues are speaking together in their native language and you simply can't understand what is being discussed. Not only is there the real insecurity that people are speaking negatively about you, but also the limitation of being excluded from meaningful conversation that limits us as leaders. There is almost certainly more creativity and synergy going on in those native language conversations than if they have to switch to English to meet your needs.

We cannot lead people to the highest levels until we know them at the deepest levels.

Language is much more emotional, more fundamental for us than we might imagine. We at Bilingual America see it in our leadership training work with Latinos, even with bilingual Latinos—when the training is done in Spanish, we achieve much better results because we're able to work on a much deeper emotional path.

A client who is a paramedic for Universal Studios in Orlando, Florida, confirmed this. He told me there are cases when Hispanic people who go into trauma revert back to their native language; they literally cannot speak English (even though under normal conditions they are able to do so). Our native language is our default language in times of great emotion or shock. It's the language of our dreams, our deepest hopes and fears. The greater your fluency in someone's language, the greater your mutual understanding and influence. Leaders who develop the language skills of the people with whom they work will always be able to connect more deeply, and this will improve their ability to motivate and lead.

2. History

History is the story of how we got to where we are. You can't understand people in the present unless you understand their past.

In the United States there are many cultural groups, but there are only a handful of categories that receive primary attention nationally and corporately. These are Hispanics, African Americans, Native Americans, Asians, Muslims, the LGBTQ+ community, and as of this writing, even Millennials.

You can't understand people in the present unless you understand their past.

If you think of the people you are leading or working with in terms of these broad groups, you might very well resist learning this history altogether. Who can learn all of Asian history? All of Latin American history?

Take a deep breath and think a little more deeply. Push yourself, first of all, to get a little more specific. Are your "Latino" colleagues of Mexican heritage? Or Chilean? Big difference! Are your "Asian" workers Vietnamese? or Japanese? Big difference!

Now that you are more clear about who your people are, what can you learn about their history? What have been their main concerns from a societal standpoint? What have been their most painful experiences with those outside their groups? (This is important, because most counter-movements are born out of pain.) What events do they commemorate or celebrate?

You may be thinking, But I hated history in school! Fortunately, now you have a better motivation. Think about it this way: How can we effectively negotiate with, sell to, create with, partner with, or work with people whom we know nothing, or very little, about? It is next to impossible.

How do you learn about their history? The answer: Study. Learn. Then learn some more. The number one skill of great negotiators is knowledge of their counterparts. Notice I didn't say *enemies*. As Steven Covey writes, our goal is "the win–win."

Your study of history can help you get to the deep structures of the culture, like its values, beliefs, and attitudes. So as you study, keep asking the deeper questions. If you're studying a particular war, for example, ask things like how might this war have affected people's belief and trust in their leaders? Their feelings of patriotism? Their attitudes toward government? Their attitudes toward your culture or country? The deeper you go, the deeper you'll know.

3. Major political or movement leaders

There's a fun little exercise I do in my live "Success with Hispanics" seminars. I put up a picture of President Barack

Obama and a picture of President Donald Trump. Once everyone in the room is finished being upset for one reason or another, I ask them, "Who are these two people?" They reply dutifully, "Two presidents of the United States."

Perfect. *Perfecto.*

Then I put up two more pictures: The men who were the *presidentes* of Mexico during President Obama's and President Trump's tenure. I ask the audience for their names. Although I am speaking to a group of leaders who employ a significant number of Mexican Americans in their workforce, most have no idea who the present or past presidents of Mexico are. They certainly would have no idea whether or not one of them is liberal or conservative. It happens every time—very few of them know who these guys are or what they stand for.

How do we lead people from other countries when we don't know the most basic facts about their major leaders? We can expect people from other countries to know something about George Washington, Abraham Lincoln, John F. Kennedy, Martin Luther King Jr., Ronald Reagan, Barack Obama, Hillary Clinton, and Donald Trump. As leaders, shouldn't we know at least some basic facts about the leaders of the movements or countries from which our associates come?

4. Sports icons (past and present)

Michael Jordan, Magic Johnson, Muhammad Ali, Babe Ruth, Hank Aaron, Peyton Manning, Tom Brady, Steph Curry, LeBron James. These are all very well-known American sports icons. Many of us feel that they are an important part of our lives too.

Well, the same is true for people in other countries or cultures.

Wayne Rooney is just as important to Brits as Peyton Manning is to many Americans.

Leonel Messi is probably even more important to Argentinians than LeBron James is to Americans.

These feelings about sports icons are present in nearly every culture. Sports shape culture, and they shape people. I grew up idolizing Roberto Clemente. I still frequently wear a hat that bears the Puerto Rican flag and his number—21. I was 12 when Roberto Clemente died on New Year's Eve, 1972, while flying to Nicaragua to offer relief to earthquake victims. I still remember that night and the deep emotions I felt. I find it more than fitting that his last hit in Major League Baseball was his 3,000th, and to me, he forever defines the 3,000-hit club. By the way, if you want to make a hit with me, start a conversation about Clemente.

Every cultural master should know something about the most popular sports and the most important sports figures of the cultures they are working with.

Let's play a little game. Look at the names below and identify the culture each athlete is associated with. Just fill in the blanks. The answers are at the back of the book, in the appendix.

Roberto Clemente   _____

(OK, I was just spotting you points there.)

Memo Ochoa   _____

Leonel Messi   _____

Fernando Valenzuela   _____

Greg Louganis   _____

Rory McElroy   _____

Steffi Graff   _____

Billy Jean King   _____

Cristiano Ronaldo   _____

Miguel Cabrera   _____

Yao Ming   _____

You get the point. People of different cultures tend to identify with athletes who most represent them, their country, their city, or their group. You need to know who they are.

5. Major landmarks

The world is a big and beautiful place, and every country has its sights of wonder. People who come from other countries and cultures are proud of the sites of natural beauty and the man-made icons of their home countries.

If you are working with people from China, can you name the most amazing landmarks to view and experience there (other than the Great Wall)? Or let's say you work with people from Mexico. Do you know whether Mazatlán is a modern suburb of Mexico City or a colonial city away from it all? (Just to help you out here, it is a colonial city on the Pacific Coast southwest of Durango and northwest of Zacatecas.) Knowing some of the landmarks that the people you work with cherish is one way to show respect for their culture.

6. Musical artists and types of music

Music is a reflection of the soul. If you are working with British people, you would know The Beatles, The Rolling Stones, Pink Floyd, Led Zeppelin, Elton John, Cat Stevens,

Adele, and David Bowie. These are British cultural icons and also household names in the United States.

If you are working with Colombian people, you may know artists such as Shakira and Carlos Vives. Would you know others equally important to the Colombian people, such as El Grupo Niche, La Sonora Carruseles, among others?

If you are working with primarily evangelical Christian people, it would be helpful to know artists such as Fanny Crosby, Bill Gaither, John W. Peterson, Keith Green, Steven Curtis Chapman, BeBe and CeCe Winans, and Michael W. Smith, among others.

In the United States, we pretty much know the difference between rock, country, jazz, hip-hop, R&B, blues, and so on. You probably even know that within each of these genres there are subgenres—for example, heavy metal, classic rock, hard rock, soft rock, Southern rock, and more, right? But would you know the musical genres of Latin music? There is salsa, bachata, cumbia, merengue, rock Latino, reggaetón, balada, norteña, mariachi, folklórica, vallenato, and many more. The music of other cultures may be even more complex and varied than American music.

To some degree, every culture is defined by its music. As a cultural master, you will need to learn the most important and influential musical artists and their works if you want to master an understanding of a given culture and connect with its people. With Latinos, you may even want to take some dance lessons!

7. Food

If music is the reflection of a culture's soul, then food *is* the soul of a culture. Food is an integral cultural element—food is art, it is the external expression of the heart.

Enjoy the food—this is a fun step! Learning about a culture's cuisine might start with something as simple as discovering the best *real* Mexican food in your city. (By the way, in many U.S. cities there are some Mexican restaurants that serve Americanized Mexican food during the week but on Sundays they serve authentic Mexican food, since that is typically when Mexicans go out with their families for a meal.)

As I was learning about Mexican food and history, I discovered something really delicious about Mazatlán, the coastal city I mentioned in the landmarks section. It turns out that Mazatlán is considered the shrimp capital of the world! So, if you're looking for a nice colonial town on the beach with incredible shrimp, this may just be the place for you. Personally, give me those enticing little creatures grilled and then coated with coconut and mango sauce. (Of course, that's the Puerto Rican in me wanting those tropical flavors.)

Once you've started frequenting your hometown's best spots for the authentic food of the culture you're studying, you'll want to learn more. For example, what are the key ingredients, and how are they grown and prepared? Take the simple egg. In France, each individual egg is stamped with the date the hen laid it, so the buyer knows exactly when to use it for maximum flavor. When you learn something like this about an ingredient, you can start to think about how a seemingly insignificant element like an egg works differently in that culture than in your own. How is the French dating system different from in the United States, where we have expiration dates? Might this tell us something about French values and attitudes about food?

Why is it important to understand the food of a culture? Why should you do your menu planning homework if you are hosting visitors from another country? Because it shows that you have taken a step toward learning about their culture. And that, in turn, is a step in respectful cultural mastery. For example, is the Happy Family Stir-Fry menu item really Chinese, or is it an American twist on Chinese food? Do you know? Does it matter? It does if you are talking with a Chinese associate, partner, team member, or friend about Chinese cuisine.

Do you know the most famous chefs of a given culture? Do you know the most beloved dishes or recipes from within a given culture? If you work closely with people from that culture, it behooves you to learn!

Of course, we don't have to stop at learning these seven elements. Learning about major writers, scientists, civic leaders, filmmakers, and others is all part of educating ourselves about a given culture. And as we've seen, learning about the surface elements can start to teach us about a culture's deeper structure—its attitudes, beliefs, and values. One of the most exciting things in life is learning new things. And it never ends. Even when you get to Stage Six, you'll still want to be learning. The Six Stages of Cultural Mastery, although presented in a linear manner, do have some wonderful interplay.

The Benefits of Cultural Education

The learning I have just described may seem challenging. Why would you want to learn so much about someone else's culture? Because you want multiple points of communication and commonality with the people you lead. In Spanish the word *comunicación* begins with the root word *común*, which means "common" in English. The most effective communication takes place when we discover and work together on the things we have in common.

When you have the knowledge to start creating commonalities with people of other cultures, they will start to view you as someone who values them. You'll be in a much better position to create positive, productive, and yes, more profitable working relationships.

When you can speak intelligently with people about things that matter to them, your likelihood of being able to connect with them, influence them, and make an impact on their lives increases exponentially.

When you can speak intelligently with people about things that matter to them, your likelihood of being able to connect with them, influence them, and make an impact on their lives increases exponentially.

Your willingness to learn shows that you care. It shows that you've taken the time to get to know them and their people.

Education is the first stage of cultural mastery.

Resources

- **Learning a language:** Of course, the best place to learn Spanish or English (for native Spanish speakers) is Bilingual America (bilingualamerica.com). If you desire to learn a different language, let us know and we'll try to send you down the right path. In the interest of transparency, I am the founder and CEO of Bilingual America.

- **Places to start your cultural learning:** If you're a reader, visit your public library or bookstore, browse online stores like Amazon, Barnes & Noble, and Powell Books, or go directly to publishers that specialize in your culture. For online learning, visit sites like Khan Academy (khanacademy.org); edX (edx.org), which offers nearly 200 courses in history alone; or Carnegie Mellon's Open Learning Initiative (oli.cmu.edu/learn-with-oli/see-our-free-open-courses/), which includes language courses. And that's just the beginning of what you can do.

- **Ethnic Food Guides:** In his *Food Lover's Guide to the World* Mark Bittman helps us experience great cuisines from around the globe. *National Geographic* has published a wonderful book titled *Food Journeys of a Lifetime: Extraordinary Places to Eat around the Globe*. You can find both at Amazon.com.

 STAGE TWO

Engagement

Once we accept our limits, we go beyond them.

—ALBERT EINSTEIN

ANJEZË GONXHE BOJAXHIU WAS born into a Kosovar Albanian family in what is today Skopje, Macedonia. Her father died when she was just eight years old. By the time she was 12, she had committed herself to religious life and missionary service. Even as a child, she knew that she wanted to engage with people of different cultures. In 1928, at the age of 18, she left home to become a postulant and learn English in a Loreto convent in Ireland. She took the name Teresa. The following year Sister Teresa was sent to India, where she learned Bengali in Darjeeling, at the foot of the Himalayan mountains.

Teresa became a teacher and eventually the headmistress at the Loreto convent school in Calcutta, India. One day in 1946, while on a train, she experienced what she called "the call within the call." Violence, famine, and abject poverty in Calcutta was weighing heavily on Teresa's soul at the time. The call she heard was to leave the convent and, as she put it, "help the poor while living among them." She was called to engage further. And because Mother Teresa engaged, Calcutta and millions of people beyond Calcutta were influenced in ways no one could ever have imagined.

Unbeknown to Teresa at the time, that experience would propel her to take Indian citizenship, start a school, solicit for supplies and funds, and found the Missionaries of Charity, an order devoted to helping "the poorest of the poor." In 1997 the world lost a truly caring and engaged human being when Teresa passed away. Today we know her as an icon of empathy and endearment, the highly revered Saint Teresa. On September 4, 2016, Pope Francis beatified Teresa in Saint Peter's Square in Vatican City, Rome, thus bestowing on her the highest honor in the Catholic Church. What's instructive for us is that she started this journey as an impoverished nun, a foreigner, a pilgrim on the Six Stages.

Everyone has a calling, or mission. If you truly embrace your calling, you will need to engage at deeper levels than the average person. Again, *we cannot lead people to the highest levels until we know them at the deepest levels.*

My calling is to bring together people of differing cultural backgrounds for the common good. Back in the late 1990s, when I started getting serious about teaching cultural relationships between Latinos and non-Latinos in the United States, I realized that I must first, as Einstein said, "accept my limits and go beyond them." I had to engage.

Although people of Mexican heritage compose around 67 percent of the Latino population in the United States, and although I am myself of Hispanic heritage as a Puerto Rican, I hadn't engaged much with people in the Mexican community at that time. I knew a lot of facts (I had entered Stage One) but I didn't understand them firsthand. This was a real limitation for me. I had never truly engaged, and I felt I needed to do so.

At that time I was living in the Atlanta, Georgia, area, attending frequent Latino business get-togethers and conducting some focus groups with Mexicans in client companies. I decided to get a PhD. in Mexican studies. I was going to master this no matter what.

Now, this wasn't a typical academic PhD. program—this was a Pool Hall Degree! I bought a pool table, put it in my living room and practiced and practiced so I could engage with Mexicans in their pool halls on the weekends without embarrassing myself. People often speak more authentically in bars and places like pool halls than in more formal settings. It is not my intent to offend anyone here, but most people go to pool halls to drink and play pool. Frequently I engaged in conversations with people who had had more than a few drinks, and they became quite talkative as a result.

By engaging with Mexican workers, and eventually Central American workers, in this environment I learned more than I could ever have learned in a classroom. We were open and honest with one another; they would share things with me that I don't think I could have learned, or felt, anywhere else.

What Is Cultural Engagement?

No doubt you are familiar with the concept of engagement in terms of relationships—it's the period of time before marriage in which the couple continues to get to know each other but at a much deeper and more personal level. Engagement is also designed to create an interval between the initial commitment and a total commitment. Engagement allows couples the opportunity to get close enough to each other to determine whether or not they want to make a long-term commitment. If the engagement period doesn't go well, things will likely end between them, and they will never get beyond this stage.

Similarly, cultural engagement allows us to deepen the understanding about a given culture that we've started in Stage

One. It lets us strengthen and even test our commitment to a relationship with this culture. It brings us closer to the people we lead. As we learn to effectively engage, we give ourselves the best possible chance for successful relationships with those from other cultures.

> *As we learn to effectively engage, we give ourselves the best possible chance for successful relationships with those from other cultures.*

Three Barriers to Cultural Engagement

Being culturally engaged is not always easy, and it doesn't come naturally to all people. In fact, many people find it easier to operate in a *dis*engaged mode; it is less risky and doesn't require the mental, emotional, and sometimes physical stretch that true engagement requires. The three main barriers to cultural engagement are fear, prejudice, and pain.

Fear

Honestly, it was scary the first time I walked into a Mexican pool hall. It was about 11 p.m. on a Saturday night in Atlanta, at a place on Buford Highway. Guys were talking loudly, some were drunk, and here I was, this white guy (they didn't know then that I was Puerto Rican) walking into their world. I'm sure many thought, *Ay, Dios mio*, it's *la migra!* Although I walked in with some trepidation, I didn't let fear keep me from engaging. I quickly found someone to talk with and started speaking Spanish with him, laughing and being friendly, so the others would know things were *tranquilo*.

You might be thinking, No way would I do that! I understand. I am not timid by nature, but I do understand that many people struggle to engage with *any* new person, even with people who look like them, speak their language, and share their culture. For some, timidity drives their fear and behavior, and this fear needs to be actively confronted in order to engage in a meaningful manner.

For starters, realize that how you engage should suit your personality and your situation. Not everyone would choose to enter a Mexican pool hall late at night in a Latino barrio. The key is to learn to engage in ways that are both meaningful and doable for you (though I would encourage you to stretch yourself).

Sometimes people are called, as Mother Teresa was, to engage on a very intense, even dangerous level. Malala Yousafzai had every right to fear for her life while growing up in Pakistan. Her father, Ziauddin, ran a school in Swat, Pakistan, and was a strong advocate for quality education for children. But the Taliban strongly opposed education for young girls and violent attacks on schools were not uncommon. (Pakistan has the third-highest percentage of unschooled children in the world, and over 60 percent of these are girls[5].) In 2009, Malala began writing a blog (under a pseudonym) for BBC Urdu (British Broadcasting Corporation) regarding her fears that her school would be attacked by the Taliban. As things became more tense in the region, women were banned from going shopping in public and Malala's father was told to close the school.

---

5 "Girls' Education in Pakistan," Global Campaign for Education website, campaignforeducation.org.

Malala kept writing, and along with her father, continued to speak out publicly against this injustice. On October 9, 2012, a masked gunman from the Taliban entered the bus on which Malala rode to school, asked for her by name and took one direct shot at her that went through her head, neck, and shoulder. Miraculously, the 15-year-old survived the shot and after three months of medical care, was released from the hospital.

Fear never dissuaded Malala. She knew her life was in danger but she kept writing, she kept advocating for justice, women's rights, and equality in education. In 2014, she became the youngest person ever to receive the Nobel Peace Prize. Though still a target of evil, she remains fully and totally engaged for the good of Pakistani children.

Malala's experience is a pretty extreme example of engagement. I am not suggesting that you should engage at that depth, nor am I suggesting that you should not. I am simply asking you to consider your fear in light of her experience, and Teresa's.

> *The more deeply we engage, the more influence we can have.*

If either of them had succumbed to their fear, it could have sabotaged a very important life mission. How you engage, and the level of your engagement, is your decision only. My point is that the more deeply we engage, the more influence we can have.

Fear is life's greatest obstacle to success and progress. It can even become a self-fulfilling prophecy, bringing about the very thing you fear. If you fear never being able to authentically connect with people who are different from you, then you likely never will: Your internal fear will make this an external reality.

Another type of fear many people experience is called *xeno-phobia*. This word was chosen as Dictionary.com's Word of the Year in 2016 due to the high number of searches it recorded during the Brexit vote and the controversial U.S. presidential campaigns. The word is a compound composed of "xénos" (foreigner) and "phobia" (fear). So it literally means "fear of foreigners." Of course, it is not always actual foreigners that people fear—it is their customs, the surface, and the deep elements of their cultural icebergs. These cultural differences can be so acute that they feel threatening to one's sense of self, and in the worst cases, to one's existence. (Icebergs colliding.)

We can experience xenophobia even in our own country. In large multiethnic countries such as the United States, it is also possible to feel like a foreigner even if you are a citizen born and bred. For example, if you are from Birmingham, Alabama, and you travel to Boston, Massachusetts, you may very well feel like you're in another country. If you were raised in Ankeny, Iowa, you'll feel like you're in another country the first time you travel one state over and visit the South Side of Chicago.

Xenophobia cuts both ways. Many times, the very people who are most prone to call others xenophobic are just as xenophobic themselves. Calling another person a xenophobe does absolutely nothing to dissuade them from being fearful. It simply creates more animosity and division, and leaves that person even less able to form a positive relationship with the people they fear. Their fear is real and should be respected for what it is. The only way to dissuade them from their fear is to first recognize its reality without judging the fear or the person who is fearful. Then, and only then, can we embark on a path of education and engagement that will allow people to see clearly whether their fear (which is perceived as real) is founded or unfounded.

Thankfully, many fearful people who are properly educated about and engaged with persons from a foreign culture will change their views about that culture. Thus, the first two stages can help eliminate fear. One thing is for sure: Insulting people, ridiculing them, or shaming them for their very real fear will have no positive effect at all, and more important, it will leave them unable to form positive relationships with the very people for whom you are advocating.

Fear is fear. It is a feeling—it has a cause. It is not our job as Cultural Masters to judge anyone's fear, not even our own. We must accept reality before we can confront reality, and for a lot of people, fear is a very real reality. To diminish fear, we must learn and engage. We must face our own realities and work through our own fears before we can gently and thoughtfully help others face theirs.

Prejudice

To be prejudiced about someone or something simply means *to prejudge*. We all do it. We make assumptions about people before we know them, assumptions that may or may not be true.

Most of our prejudices are based on our own (limited) experiences or on things we see or hear from others, but also including memes and images from media like movies, TV, and books. This is typical. All people, I am convinced, carry such prejudices. Often our prejudices are based on stereotypes: limited, often false ideas or images of people that we pick up from our

culture and experience. If we see multiple negative or derogatory images of people who belong to a certain group in media
such as ads or movies—we might apply that negativity to the
actual people we meet who are from the same culture. Or our
prejudice appears when we have a negative experience, like
someone cutting us off in line at the grocery store. If the person
involved is from a different culture, we attach that poor behavior to their culture. That's prejudice. It can happen incredibly
fast, without conscious thought. And the more we do it without
paying attention to it, the more our prejudice grows.

If we allow our prejudices to control our thinking and our
behavior, we will never engage with people in an open and
transparent way. Engagement will simply be impossible. As we
have already seen, it is impos-
sible to effectively engage with
or lead people if we are resisting them emotionally, and
this includes being prejudiced
toward them.

> *If we allow our prejudices
> to control our thinking and
> our behavior, we will never
> engage with people in an
> open and transparent way.*

As you begin to engage, you don't have to convince yourself from the get-go that your prejudice is wrong (or right). You
simply have to convince yourself to put your prejudice(s) aside
until you find out more about how things really are. You may
find that you have a selective prejudice based on a small sample
size and that the macro culture doesn't fit into that little box.
The more you can replace negative images with positive images,
the greater your resilience against prejudice will be.

Pain

It makes sense that the mother of a child killed by an intoxicated driver would have strong negative opinions about drunk drivers, right? Similarly, it makes sense that the father of a son killed by a man who came into a country illegally would have strong negative opinion about everyone who entered the country illegally. Would you expect such a mother to engage with alcoholics, or such a father to engage with undocumented immigrants? Probably not. But if they did, their experience would be certain to transform their suffering.

One of the most difficult things to do in life is to engage with people who have hurt us deeply. We want to get those people out of our lives, not bring them closer. Thus, pain and loss can keep us from moving forward in life. Their paralyzing emotions can keep us from engaging, from seeing

> *One of the most difficult things to do in life is to engage with people who have hurt us deeply.*

people as they truly are, or can be, rather than through the lens of our hurt.

As leaders of organizations or businesses, perhaps we, or someone we care about, has been hurt by someone from a particular culture, and it's understandable if this makes us reticent to engage with anyone from that culture. (I wonder if Mr. Sproul, the gentleman I mentioned earlier who gave me such a ringing endorsement when I spoke in Phoenix, may have been burdened with such an experience when I met him.) Hurt can keep us from engaging, thus circumventing any hope of us ever to become Cultural Masters capable of effectively leading people from different cultures and backgrounds.

If this applies to you, remember that we humans have a long history of working through our hurt to a greater good. Pain, historically speaking, is behind almost every great social and civic movement. If you can find a way to set aside your hurt about that experience long enough to learn a little about one brilliant person from that culture, or a little bit of history, eventually you'll find that you want to engage with actual people. And before you know it, you'll be on your way toward letting go of your limiting, inhibiting pain and being truly transformed.

Three Actions to Help You Engage

How do we engage? Allow me to remind you that three of the Six Stages of Cultural Mastery require proactive behavior on our part, and this is one of them. Yes, it takes real commitment to engage with other people. It takes energy. It takes time. Sometimes it takes downright courage. However, if we are leading people of other cultures, this is part of our responsibility—and the benefits of engagement are significant.

Following are three principles that will help you engage in a way that will be meaningful—both for you and for those with whom you engage:

1. Prepare

Before you go out trying to engage with people, prepare yourself. This also takes us back to Stage One: Education. In my case, I prepared by buying a pool table so I could get good enough to be respected in the pool hall.

So if you want to engage with, say, a group of businesspeople from the Makah Indian Reservation in Washington State, you might prepare by learning about Makah history and culture, about landmarks like Tatoosh Island, about fishing and whaling, about Ozette Village and the Makah Research and Cultural Center. You might learn a few words of the Makah language. And you should learn something about treaty and fishing rights. That's just a start.

2. Practice

That's right, practice. I practiced pool for countless hours. I didn't want to embarrass myself or count myself out of the opportunity to play with someone I wanted to speak with or get to know.

Practice is part of the training process. When we learn to ride a bicycle we are taught using training wheels. These wheels keep us from tipping over while we are learning to keep our balance. They are just above the actual line of the two main wheels so that as we gain our balance, the training wheels only serve as the lifelines until we fully master the skill.

If you're learning a new language and you want to use it in real and meaningful situations, naturally you'll want to practice it with a professional instructor beforehand. If you want to engage for the first time with a group of people in their social setting, you'll want to practice first, perhaps by getting together with the one among them you are most comfortable with.

For example, let's say you are planning to engage by attending a meeting of your local Asian Pacific Chamber of Commerce. Perhaps consider finding someone within that community who will role-play some different possible scenarios with you. In addition to learning about the main players and mission of the association (Stage One: Education), role-playing some scenarios will give you practice in applying what you have learned. If you have to, get in front of a mirror and practice what you are going to say. How do Asians typically great each other? What are protocols for entering or leaving a conversation? Remember, communication is both verbal and nonverbal, and it helps to know when to keep quiet. (Listening is a skill that takes practice as well.) Another way to practice might be to visit a similar group away from your home area where you can practice without so much at stake. This would be akin to a professional sports teams playing an exhibition game. The point is that engagement can be practiced, so when you get to the real deal, you're ready. And remember, even when you do get to the real deal, at least at the beginning you'll be a rookie, so be patient with yourself and keep practicing! You'll be in the major leagues soon.

3. Participate

Once you prepare and practice, it's time to participate. At this point, you should have the skill and confidence to engage in a self-assured and meaningful way.

One thing I have found is that people who are different (that is, from other cultures), are almost always very impressed when we take the time to participate in their activities in an educated and meaningful way. The problem is that most people don't prepare and practice beforehand, and then they don't (or can't) understand why people are not responding to them the way they had hoped. So before you participate, prepare and practice! And then be open to what happens—try to loosen up on your expectations. Granted, this takes a bit of humility on the front end but it's more than worth it, since people will clearly see that your heart and soul is with them.

The Benefits of Cultural Engagement

Engagement takes commitment. Yes, we may be fearful, we may carry prejudices or, unfortunately, deep pain within us, but as leaders we commit to working through challenges for the overall good of our calling and mission.

The beauty of the engagement period is that it also produces some real anticipation and promise for the future. Engagement may be the toughest of the Six Stages but it is the one and only stage that can move us forward to the critical stage of Empathy. It is impossible to feel deeply or passionately for another person, or group of people, without having authentically engaged with them first.

Resources

- **Prejudice:** Project Implicit offers an intriguing, scientific approach to prejudice and bias. Project Implicit "translates academic research into practical applications for addressing diversity, improving decision making, and increasing the likelihood that practices are aligned with personal and organizational values." The website, implicit.harvard.edu/implicit/, offers some fascinating quizzes you can take to measure your unconscious bias about factors like race and mental illness.

- **Fear:** Dr. John Powell's book, *Why Am I Afraid to Tell You Who I Am?* changed my life. It is written from a Christian perspective, but the truths will apply no matter your religious backgrounds or beliefs. I highly recommend it to you.

- **Measuring Cultural Engagement:** Sponsored by the National Endowment for the Arts and Arts and Humanities Research Council, this 60-page report seeks to identify new terms, tools, and techniques for cultural engagement. You can download the report here: rts.gov/sites/default/files/measuring-cultural-engagement.pdf

STAGE THREE

Empathy

I think we all have empathy.
We may not have enough courage to display it.

—MAYA ANGELOU

ASHLEY JIRÓN, OWNER OF P.B. Jams Café in Oklahoma City, Oklahoma, noticed that someone was going through the café's dumpster and opening bags of trash. Ashley assumed it was a homeless person seeking something to eat. Rather than reporting this person to the police or asking someone else to take care of it, she left the following note:

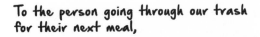

To the person going through our trash for their next meal,

You're a human being and worth more than a meal from a dumpster. Please come in during operating hours for a classic Pb&j, fresh veggies and a cup of water at no charge. No questions asked.

—Your friend the owner.

I was moved when I first saw this on a web-based news feed, so I did a quick search to find out more about Ashley and her business. One restaurant guide said that the business was closed, which I found odd—usually people who demonstrate this type of goodness prosper in business.

I decided to call the business simply to find out if it was indeed closed. When a woman answered the phone I asked, "What are your hours today?" She said that they were closed due to a fire that had destroyed the property just three days before. She seemed a bit emotional, so following a hunch I asked her if she was Ashley. She said she was. Trying to be sensitive, and knowing that she was in the midst of fire inspectors, insurance adjusters, and the like, I explained that I was doing research for this book and had read about her act of kindness. She was kind enough to talk with me, and during the conversation it came out that the café had fed not only that one homeless person, but several hundred others as well.

Ashley is one empathetic person.

One thing is for sure—the next time I am in Oklahoma City, the first place I am going is P.B. Jams for a delicious peanut butter-and-jelly sandwich. Ashley has earned my support and admiration. (Oh, by the way, when she gave me her email address and said her last name, it sounded as if she was of Latino descent. So I asked her if she had a Latino background. She laughed nervously and made a comment about not speaking Spanish well, since she is from a multigenerational Mexican American family. Without a doubt, my company, Bilingual America, will be providing Ashley with Spanish training at no charge if she wants to learn!)

Empathy is key to cultural mastery; in fact, Stage Three is the tipping point stage. Without true empathy, we cannot get to the subsequent stages.. And the good news is that we can learn it.

Our Struggles Can Teach Us Empathy

Perhaps one of the best examples of the absolute importance of empathy comes from Dr. Wayne Dyer's book *Inspiration*, in which he tells the story of how he embarked on a mission to help people forgive and redeem one another.[6]

The following is my paraphrase of Dr. Dyer's story:

Before I came to Earth, God asked me what I wanted to accomplish during my lifetime there. I told him that I wanted to teach forgiveness and redemption. He asked me if I was sure, to which I replied that I was absolutely sure.

He said okay and then proceeded to inform me that in order to teach forgiveness and redemption I would need to personally learn and experience them.

He told me I would be born into a disadvantaged family and my father would abandon my brother and me. He said that when I learned to forgive my father for this I could then teach forgiveness.

He continued and said that my mother's poverty would be so deep that she wouldn't be able to support my brother and me and we would live in and out of foster homes for many years. He said that my mother would work and struggle to get her life together to the point where she could redeem us out of that cycle, and that when she did, I could then teach redemption.

---

6   Dr. Wayne W. Dyer, *Inspiration: Your Ultimate Calling*, Hay House, 2006.

His complete story is more detailed and powerful—I highly recommend it. What is the bottom line for our purposes? Dr. Dyer learned to be passionate about helping other people experience forgiveness and redemption in their lives only *because he experienced the need for these things at the deepest personal level.* He developed true empathy because of his own life engagement with these deeply personal matters.

Dr. Dyer's story transformed my view of my own life and mission. I read it on an airplane on my way to California to give a series of speeches. I was traveling with my oldest daughter, Andrea. While reading this story, I started to cry, and Andrea asked me why I was crying. I replied that it was the first time I deeply understood and started to accept my own mixed heritage. I had struggled my entire life with accepting my mother's deep Southern roots. For reasons I didn't understand in my youth, I had very little empathy for that particular culture, to put it lightly. I resisted it emotionally, and I'd spent my life trying to distance myself from it, and in consequence, I was rejecting part of myself, as well as sabotaging my very mission to bring together people of different cultures and backgrounds.

As I read this story I understood that I was placed into a very difficult bicultural childhood so that I could have true empathy for people on both sides of the cultural narrative. Embracing both sides of my heritage was a critical piece of my healing; it helped me become whole and freed me to have a positive voice for all cultures, not simply my chosen one. I can honestly say that now I am able to work with people of multiple cultures without bias for one or another. I simply want to help people find the common good. When I watch people of different backgrounds and cultures learn to work together in positive ways, a deep sense of gratitude, and perhaps personal redemption, wells up inside me. Because I know firsthand the power of empathy.

What Is Empathy?

I cannot speak modern Greek, but I had five years of training in Koine New Testament Greek. The word *empathy* is a composite of two Greek words: *em* (in) and *pathos* (passion). Empathy is not simply an expression of concern or kindness. Empathy is not sympathy. (And if we're honest, we'll recognize that many of our modern-day social programs are based on sympathy.) Empathy is a state of being *passionate* about other people.

Are you passionate about the people you lead or influence? If you are truly empathetic, you live "in passion" with those around you. Empathy is not simply an expression of concern or kindness, it is a state of passionate being. As British Pakistani novelist Mohsin Hamid so beautifully wrote, "Empathy is about finding echoes of another person in yourself."

Empathy is the stage in which negative bias is replaced with positive bias.

When we have true empathy and are deeply passionate about other people, we see their talents, abilities, skills, and more. We see them in a positive light. Empathy is the stage in which negative bias is replaced with positive bias. We cannot maintain negative bias against someone with whom we are truly empathetic.

This is critical. There is so much talk of unconscious bias and conscious bias, implicit bias and explicit bias. But even when I become conscious of my unconscious bias, or when my implicit bias becomes explicit, I still have bias. Negative bias can only be replaced with positive bias, and empathy is the key.

Three Barriers to Empathy

As with all stages of development, there are walls or barriers we must scale in order to get to a state of empathy for those we lead. You may have noticed that empathy is an internal issue of the heart. It is not something we *do*, it is something that grows out of educating ourselves and engaging meaningfully with others different from ourselves.

So what are the roadblocks to empathy? What keeps us from being passionate about and for other people? Lack of passion, impatience, and a judgmental spirit.

1. Lack of Passion

Passion—or *pathos*—is a fire within our soul. Some people do not have a passion for life itself, much less for other people. The first barrier to being passionate about other people is not having passion for life itself. In the same way that you cannot love others if you don't love yourself, you can't be passionate about others if you're not passionate about life.

I don't want to simplify this barrier. If you're stumped by something deeper in life, it's worth investigating. A long-standing lack of passion can signify depression. It can mean you're in the wrong line of work. It can point to an unresolved conflict or trauma from your past, or a spiritual wounding or need. If you feel that you have lost (or never had) passion for life, if you've spent ages on Stages One and Two and they have left you cold, then pause here and look into the cause. We are created for passion; don't settle for a passionless life.

> The first barrier to being passionate about other people is not having passion for life itself.

2. Impatience

The second barrier to empathy is impatience. We'd like to get to the destination of cultural mastery without going through the necessary stages of education and engagement. Sorry, it just doesn't happen that way. I have seen people beat themselves up emotionally because they don't have deep feelings for other people—they *want* to care, but they don't. They are impatient. They want something they cannot have because they don't have the patience to go through the necessary process to get there.

If this sounds like you, take a deep breath. Recommit yourself to the process, and "try, try again." As the saying goes, "Patience is companion to wisdom." And it takes patience, and practice, to achieve it.

Here are a few tips for developing patience on your road to cultural mastery.

- *Look at your triggers.* Is there a certain element of Stage One or Two that make you impatient? Try to pin down exactly where you get stuck. Maybe you've been trying to read a long book of history, and you just can't get into it. Or maybe you're practicing engagement and facing resistance. It just doesn't seem to be happening. Or it could be that you're running up against your deeper emotional resistance to some aspect of the culture. Whatever the culprit, when you notice it, pay attention. Then you can choose how to respond or adjust.

- *Shift your perspective.* Once you've identified a trigger for your impatience, take a side step. Many people, for instance, are aural or visual learners rather than book learners. (See the Resources section at the end of this chapter for a quick assessment to find out which style is yours.) Try putting down that big tome and picking up your phone or tablet. Go to YouTube or Google and start learning there. (Of course, as with books, you'll want to consider the source of your online information when assessing it.) If you're struggling to engage with a particular group, take a step back and focus on one person. Seek out their advice and friendship and let them guide you. Whatever your trigger is, try shifting it. And in any case, you can practice patience. Maybe you just need to give it more time.

- *Mix it up, and follow your passion.* Let's say you are trying to engage with your colleagues by inviting them to drinks after work on Fridays and you haven't been able to really connect with them. It could be they're even starting to send their regrets. Don't give it up—mix it up! Think about your own character and interests in life, and shift your engagement method accordingly. Maybe you aren't at your best in a group setting and are not the life of the party. Try something else instead. If you love movies, organize a movie night at your home. If you love cooking ethnic foods, try having a tasting party. If, by chance, you have a sailboat—no brainer! Lead with your strengths, and your passions.

- *Breathe.* Even simple meditation will exercise those patience muscles. Do it every day. One technique I learned that has helped me a lot is this: Breathe into your abdomen through your nose for four seconds; hold the breath for six seconds; slowly exhale for eight seconds. At the very end of your exhale you may feel a desire to take another breath with a big release of air. Keep it slow and let it flow. This will release a lot of pent-up stress and help slow down your mind.

3. A Judgmental Spirit

The third barrier to empathy is a judgmental spirit. A judgmental spirit absolutely destroys our ability to be empathetic.

Many of us live our lives under a cloud of guilt and shame and then project this onto everyone else. We sincerely believe that everyone deserves the evil that comes their way. We believe in a strict framework of cause and effect. Our attitude is, "Somehow, someway, whatever you're going through is your own damn fault; deal with it, it's not my problem."

When we're insecure we tend to buttress our own viewpoints by being critical of others who hold an opposing viewpoint.

Thus, our inability to be challenged at the deepest level is often based on a deep insecurity. When we're insecure we tend to buttress our own viewpoints by being critical of others who hold an opposing viewpoint. We might also tend to surround ourselves with others who support our view of life. The trouble is, when we let our judgmental spirit take over, we can become very tied to our own opinions and viewpoints. We tend to be very quick to negatively stereotype people and succumb to prejudicial attitudes. This closes us off from people who are different from us—the opposite of what we're trying to do as Cultural Masters!

The Truth About Stereotypes

Let's take a minute to look at stereotypes and how they work. As we've seen earlier, stereotypes are those ideas and images that flash into our heads when we see someone different from us. They come from our own experience or from something we've seen or heard. They are a projection. They might hold a little bit of truth, but they claim to hold the whole truth. They may tell a single story, but they claim to tell the whole story. Stereotypes limit our understanding of people and thereby limit our appreciation and stifle our passion, our empathy.

Some stereotypes put people in a negative light, while others appear positive. As a Latino, I am very happy with the stereotype of the Latin lover. Is it true? Well, *¡por supuesto que sí!* Call me a Latin lover and I'll hug you and kiss you!

> *Stereotypes might hold a little bit of truth, but they claim to hold the whole truth. They may tell a single story, but they claim to tell the whole story.*

But even positive stereotypes can be inhibitors to true relationship building. For example, take the stereotype of the African American man as a good athlete. Let's say you meet a 6'6" African American male and the first question you really want to ask him is... Go ahead, just say it:

"Do you play basketball?"

If this guy happens to play, then you were lucky and should have made a bet. Even if you are correct, he may still cringe internally thinking about how predictable people are, or maybe he is just tired of getting asked this same question over and over. But what if he has never played basketball? What if he is a concert pianist? Then he would feel like you are stereotyping him in a way that just doesn't fit his reality and you would lose connection with him.

You can clearly see that adhering to even a positive stereotype can keep us from connecting at a deep personal level with people.

Other stereotypes are not so positive and cut deeply, both ways. They have the power to ruin the careers of those who express them.

A few years back, I was invited to speak at a conference about doing business with Latinos. About a week before the conference, the executive director of the association sponsoring the event called and asked me if I played golf. "Well," I told him, "I'm no Chi Chi Rodríguez, but I've been playing quite a bit and have a pretty low handicap." Once he heard this he asked me to come up early to team up with him for a golf scramble the day before the conference started.

When I got to the golf course I quickly realized two things: They were playing for quite a bit of money, and my partner really wanted to win.

We teed off, and I had a birdie on the first hole. My partner was elated. The second hole I had par and he was still happy. The third hole I had a bogey and he asked me if everything was OK. The fourth hole I had a double bogey and when I walked off the green, he looked at me and said, "Hey, I thought you said you were good. Was that just a fluke back there?"

So now I'm feeling pressure, and an amateur golfer under pressure tends to have a blow-up hole. Mine was hole #5. My tee shot went out into the woods, my second shot was horrible, and I was laying five and still on the fairway on a par four! The guy is standing about 15 feet to my left in disbelief. I get out my seven iron, take my stance, make my swing, and the ball pops up, goes off to the right, hits the cart path, and bounces out into the woods.

My partner lost it. He screamed at me, "Why in the [blankety-blank blank] don't you go back to Puerto Rico and steal hubcaps!"

There was a moment of dead silence. I was pretty surprised, I can tell you. I've learned to respond, not to react, regarding cultural matters, so I calmed myself, looked him in the eye, and asked, "You're going to attend my speech on cultural mastery tomorrow, right?" He said he was and I replied, "That's probably a good thing." That was it. We didn't discuss it again.

There is a very important lesson in this story: Whatever is inside you, and I do mean *whatever*, at some point in time, for some reason, and in some way, it will come out. And when it does, in today's world of social media and rapid reaction, it has the power to destroy you, your career, and perhaps even your company.

> *Whatever is inside you, and I do mean whatever, at some point in time, for some reason, and in some way, it will come out. And when it does, in today's world of social media and rapid reaction, it has the power to destroy you, your career, and perhaps even your company.*

You see, when we are under stress or angry or frustrated or perhaps even trying to make a joke, our subconscious beliefs or feelings may come out. This is why it is so important to work on ourselves. Every leader who desires to become a true cultural master must commit to going through a very honest internal inventory in order to insulate him or herself against this type of occurrence.

We can all think of some very high-profile people who have had their careers completely derailed due to saying or doing things that were highly offensive to other people. Think of Paula Deen, Mel Gibson, Michael Richards (Kramer from *Seinfeld*), and Donald Sterling (who lost an NBA franchise over his comments about African Americans). I can think of many others who have fallen into this trap.

I'm reminded of a person I call The Taco Mayor. Mayor Joseph Maturo of East Haven, Connecticut, made an offhanded, ill-advised remark about Latinos and paid for it in tacos.[7] East Haven was being investigated by the FBI for systemic police abuse of Latinos. Four officers were arrested for playing a role in the abuse of Latino residents and business people, so the allegations were real. When the press asked Mayor Maturo what he was going to do to help bridge the cultural gap between the city and the Latino community, his comment was, "I might have tacos when I go home, I'm not quite sure yet." Well, his office was barraged with tacos. Yes, real tacos. Thousands of tacos. *Ay, ay, ay.* A few days later, Mayor Maturo apologized, saying that his comment was caused mostly by stress.

Again, whatever is inside you, will come out—for some reason, sooner or later. May I ask, "What's inside of you?" If you want to become a cultural master, I implore you to be very serious about doing the internal work necessary so you can enjoy high levels of success with others who are unlike you,

---

7   edition.cnn.com/2012/01/26/us/connecticut-east-haven-tacos/

and insulate yourself from potential personal self-sabotage or damage.

Can stereotypes change over time? Of course. They are cultural constructs, and culture is always changing. Do you remember the stereotypical picture of a Mexican with a sombrero sitting under a cactus, lazily passing the time? I do. Whatever you think of Mexicans right now, one thing very few people in the United States believe about them is that they are lazy. Stereotypes can, in fact, be changed as culture changes; we can get rid of old ones (and come up with new ones).

Fortunately, stereotypes can also diminish as we get to know one another better. What's more, we can work on our response to stereotypes. If my leadership capacity is being hurt by a false stereotype—say, the stereotype that women do not make good executives—I can diminish the power of that stereotype with Stages One and Two. I can fill my brain with information about all the super female executives out there; I can actively engage with my female professional network and find out firsthand how awesome they are. I can put down the blinders that the stereotype creates and really see people.

No one would choose to be born into abject poverty if given the choice. Would any of us honestly choose to be born with a birth defect? Of course not. Who would choose to have a drug-addicted mother or alcoholic father? No one. Do people choose to be homeless? No, their lives spiral out of control in ways that many of the rest of us will never understand.

What we can understand, and be passionate about, is seeing every person as a valuable human being, just as Ashley Jirón did with the homeless people she fed. What we can understand is that all of us are in some way broken, we are all "at risk" in some way, and that these apparent weaknesses can lead us to the incredible power of empathy.

To go a bit deeper, no one chooses to be short, tall, black, white, brown, bald, and so on. Such characteristics are simply the reality of our lives. It is simply immoral and inhumane to hold bias against people, much less to peg them into a stereotypical hole, for something over which they have absolutely no control. No human being controls the color of their skin, their height, the slant of their eyes, whether they have great hair or no hair, where they were born, or their socio-economic class at birth.

We cannot solve the problem of suffering and evil in the world, but we can certainly learn to be empathetic toward those who suffer at the hands of people who unjustly stereotype them—no matter who they are.

Six Ways to Develop Empathy

So, how exactly do we cultivate an empathetic spirit? What are some practical suggestions to implement? As you will see, true empathy comes as a direct result of Stages One and Two, especially through meaningful engagement in Stage Two. We can't just conjure up empathy. It is the outgrowth of real relationships.

1. **Get out of the office**. This comes back to engagement. You have to get out of the office. Walk the floor; visit your employees when they are sick or write them a note expressing your care for them; love them when one of their children suffers. Say, for example, you love cooking. When a

coworker or associate is sick, perhaps make them a meal and take it to their home. This would allow you to demonstrate empathy while also leveraging your talent and passion. If you are a mechanic, perhaps offer a helping hand to someone who you know doesn't have the money to pay for a repair. These are simple, yet powerful ways to show empathy.

2. **Get your hands dirty**. This goes beyond getting out of the office—it means getting involved at a deep level. Work alongside your team; accompany them to an important event in their community; be there and be real.

The TV show *Undercover Boss* features out-of-touch bosses getting away from their "ivory tower" to feel and touch the lives of real people. Inevitably, the ones who are most changed by the experience are the leaders who go out on the fishing boat for six weeks; the bosses who go out and pick lettuce in the field with migrant workers; the ones who cut up meat in a processing plant alongside hourly workers. Check it out, and get inspired.

> *We cannot be passionate about other people when we are really only passionate about ourselves.*

3. **Humble yourself**. We've all met people in positions of influence who are arrogant and condescending. Sadly for them, they cannot become Cultural Masters until they learn humility. We cannot be passionate about other people when we are really only passionate about ourselves.

This is a cooperative we're all in together. We may have different roles, but all of our roles are important. And no one is perfect—we've all failed on multiple occasions. We all know the pain of suffering. We all are mere mortals on this journey we call life. As leaders, we are called to exemplify this universality of the human condition—we are called to serve, which means humbling ourselves and educating and elevating those under our care. True greatness comes through service. As Jesus of Nazareth said to his twelve disciples, "Whoever wants to become great among you must be your servant."[8]

4. **Take a trip**. More fun! Yes, get out of the country and experience another culture in its native state. Eat the food, listen to the music, and be a humble learner. Don't judge the culture; remember, culture just *is*. I have a home in the Dominican Republic. I can tell you firsthand that many tourists spend way too much time criticizing the local people—how they drive, the bad roads, corruption in the government, lack of detail in customer service, and so on. Don't fall into this trap when you're traveling—it will close you off emotionally from the people and what they are really about, not to mention it will keep you from enjoying yourself.

Being around Latinos in a Latin American country is different from being around Latinos in the United States. Being around Chinese people in China or Taiwan is different from being around Chinese Americans in San Francisco—and so on. Immersing yourself in the native culture offers a much deeper, participatory experience of learning and understanding than being around immigrants from that country in your home country. By the way, when you travel, do your best to branch out from the packaged tours that are designed to keep you within a safe bubble along with other travelers. Perhaps, at the very least, take the packaged tour to get a feel for the lay of the land, and then branch out on your own or in a small group of like-minded travelers.

5. **Listen carefully**. When we're talking, we're not learning. And many of us are talking, internally, even when we're listening.

Think about how you listen. Do you listen intently, to simply learn and understand? Or are you in the habit of listening while also formulating an answer or rebuttal at the same time? Many of us fall into this second category, partly because we deeply believe that conversation is a contest.

Psychologists say that being understood is the greatest human emotional need, and it's certainly something people need from their leaders. As leaders, we can't understand if we don't listen. If we engage with an attitude of needing to prove our own point, we won't really listen. As we enter conversations, or engagements, with people different from ourselves, we need to listen deeply.

Only when we listen with both our head and our heart can we develop empathy. Listening may mean actually sitting with someone and focusing on them and their story. It may mean hanging out on a busy street corner and watching the daily grind and challenges that people face. It may mean putting on some work jeans and working together with others, without saying much, to better understand their reality.

> Only when we listen with both our head and our heart can we develop empathy.

As leaders, we must be constantly asking those under our influence and care what they are *really* thinking, feeling, or processing. Let's learn to be quiet and listen carefully and without prejudice or judgment. When we do, people will tell us everything we need to know and we'll be transformed in a very meaningful way. When we are transformed, we'll be in a much better position to help transform others.

6. **Be curious**. They say curiosity killed the cat, but the *lack* of curiosity kills far more: It kills creativity and empathy. If I am curious about how other people live—without judgment—I put myself in a position to become a much more empathetic leader and person.

Consider the role of successful scientists: They may initiate a study with a theory, but if they are too locked into that theory they may miss the real science that will unfold to them. They must be curious and open to new insights and discoveries as they are pursuing their theories. That's what cultural mastery is all about.

The Benefits of Empathy

True empathy leads us to be passionate about the people we lead. And passion leads to great things. It opens us up to deeper relationships, greater opportunities we could not have foreseen, new callings and missions. When we feel empathy, things really start to happen!

Highly successful cultural leaders have a passion for the people they lead, and it begins with having empathy.

May I get curious and ask you a question? Do you have a passion for the people you lead? Do you have true empathy as described in this chapter? Are you all about growing and developing your people and their brand rather than your own? Are you a servant leader[9] who wants to make others great? Highly successful cultural leaders have a passion for the people they lead, and it begins with having empathy. When this occurs—when you are passionate about people—it leads you to the very emotive Stage Four, which is Excitement.

Resources

- **Identifying your learning style:** There are several assessments available to help you determine whether your learning style is visual, aural, written word–based, or kinesthetic. Here's one that's fast and easy: the VARK Questionnaire, available at vark-learn.com/the-vark-questionnaire/.

- **Stereotyping:** There are thousands of resources to help us understand stereotyping. Here's one that will stick with you: "The danger of a single story," a TEDTalk by Nigerian novelist Chimamanda Ngozi Adichie, available at ted.com/talks/ chimamanda_adichie_the_danger_of_a_single_story

- **Listening:** Mutual invitation is a communication process that helps people learn to listen deeply and ensures that everyone has a chance to express themselves. You can learn more at kscopeinstitute.org/mutual-invitation/.

---

9   For information about servant leadership, see the Resources section in Stage Four.

 STAGE FOUR

Excitement

*It is always with excitement that I wake up
in the morning wondering what my intuition
will toss up to me, like gifts from the sea.
I work with it and rely on it. It's my partner.*

—DR. JONAS SALK

EARLY IN 1990, PEOPLE throughout South Africa and the world anxiously awaited the release of anti-apartheid ANC leader Nelson Mandela. South African president F.W. de Klerk had indicated he would order Mandela's release, without giving a specific date. Mandela, sentenced to life in prison, had been in jail for 27 years, and the anti-apartheid, anti-separatist movement had grown to a tipping point, pushing the De Klerk regime to start dismantling apartheid.

Then, on February 10, De Klerk called a private meeting with Mandela to inform him that he would be set free the next day. Amazingly, Mandela asked to remain in prison for another week so that his staff and family could be better prepared for his release. That request was denied, and he was escorted out of prison on February 11, 1990.

After word spread that Mandela would be released, South Africa was abuzz. Everyone knew that a seismic shift in South African politics was about to happen.

Mandela had been a boxer in his youth, but that strong young man was no longer. During his decades-long imprisonment he had been subjected to hard labor in a limestone quarry and had also contracted tuberculosis. Due to the South African government's desire to marginalize Mandela during his imprisonment, no photos of him had been released to the public until just before his release. Those photos revealed a thin and graying man. Mandela had been transformed in 27 years from a rough-and-tumble boxer, always impeccably dressed for all his court dates, to a 71-year-old elder statesman.

Words like *expectation* and *anticipation* do not fully capture the moment of Mandela's release. Fifty thousand black South Africans were estimated to be present at the Grand Parade outside Cape Town's City Hall to catch a glimpse of the man and to hear him speak.

Supporters mobbed his car as it approached Cape Town. Later Mandela wrote the following regarding this experience: "People began knocking on the windows, and then on the trunk and the hood of the car. Inside it sounded like a massive hailstorm. Then people began jumping on the car in their excitement. Others began to shake it and at that moment I began to worry. I felt as though the crowd might very well kill us with their love."[10]

When Mandela finally began his speech, words of depth and wisdom flowed from his lips. "Comrades and fellow South Africans, I greet you all in the name of peace, democracy, and freedom. I stand here before you not as a prophet, but as a humble servant of you, the people. ... Today, the majority of South Africans, black and white, recognize that apartheid has no future. It has to be ended by our decisive mass action. We have waited too long for our freedom."[11] In April 1994 Nelson Mandela was elected President of South Africa.

One of the thousands touched by life under apartheid and its subsequent dismantling was my friend Arnold Dhanesar. Arnold is a third-generation Indian born in South Africa who is now a U.S. citizen. He told me with great depth of feeling how he felt segregated by apartheid, with rules such as being

10 *Long Walk to Freedom* Vol 2: 1962-1994
11 *The Sydney Morning Herald* bit.ly/2gKe65d

able to swim only at certain beaches where people of color were allowed. He also described with much pain the Group Areas Act, which forced his family to move several times because they were not allowed to stay in areas designated for other racial groups. His life was transformed when apartheid was dismantled, and President Mandela was for him a symbol of that transformation.

Arnold has been a senior-level talent executive with the World Bank, The Coca-Cola Company, and MetLife. He now swims at the beaches of the finest hotels and resorts in the world, and when he speaks of Nelson Mandela his face comes aglow with reverence and respect. Arnold has experienced firsthand the transformative power of excitement, the fourth stage of cultural mastery.

Once we go through the stages of education, engagement, and empathy, we become excited about the people we are leading—now truly *our* people. We become excited about their potential and their possibilities. And our excitement, as leaders, is in turn inspiring to our people. Not only did Mandela excite a nation, he was himself excited about the potential of his people. How many people like Arnold Dhanesar were set free to greatness by Mandela's inspiring leadership?

What Is Excitement?

Excitement comes from a late Medieval Latin word with roots in *encouragement*. Encouragement means "to give support, confidence, or hope." Excitement about our relationship together moves us to want to create vision together.

It makes sense that excitement and encouragement are linked. Great cultural leaders are great encouragers; they are positive, not negative. They find the good in people and are not judgmental.

The definition of excitement that resonates in terms of cultural mastery is a feeling of eager enthusiasm and interest. To successfully lead and work with people of different backgrounds, it's imperative that leaders take an authentic *interest* in them—what are their goals, values, and motivations? Of course, leaders must first enter the first three stages: (1) Educate themselves regarding their associates' culture, history, important events, and so on; (2) Engage with them; and (3) Develop true empathy and passion for them. When we enter the stage of excitement, we naturally dream together about the things we can

> *When we enter the stage of excitement, we naturally dream together about the things we can accomplish for the common good.*

accomplish for the common good. This is when vision and mission become embedded in our relationships.

As mentioned in the introduction, many leaders, if not most, skip Stages One through Three and want to move directly to Stage Four. They want to create a vision—and not always together. The reality is that it takes time to deeply understand and meaningfully engage with people. It's hard to propel ourselves to a real sense of passion about and admiration for people different from ourselves, and it seems easier to skip those stages. Yet ultimately it's short-sighted and limiting.

Many companies have a mission or vision statement posted somewhere on their office walls or website. They require that it be learned in the onboarding process. Unfortunately, we cannot policy culture; it grows out of meaningful relationships and true empathy for one another.

In terms of creating organizational culture, excitement is a sustained environment of encouragement and the one thing we are encouraging is the creation and implementation of shared visions. To determine whether you are mastering this stage, ask yourself: Do you always seek to find the good in your people? Do you consistently tell them about their positive qualities and strengths? Is everyone part of the vision-creating process? Does everyone in the organization have a meaningful seat at the table? So many times, a group of leaders will work together and develop a vision for reaching "other people" without even having those people at the table. This, of course, makes very little sense from a cultural standpoint. If you are excited about the people you lead, your followers will also get excited about you, your leadership, and your shared mission.

They will feel welcome. Even more than welcome—they will feel they are an intrinsic part of the process, encouraged and expected to share their creative suggestions and talents. Excitement about each other is a kind of positive bias—an expectation of good things from each other that's based on knowledge and shared experience.

Three Barriers to Excitement

Staying excited and enthusiastic has its challenges. For example, we cannot excite others if we are not excited about our own life, purpose, and mission. I have found that the three main barriers that leaders face in creating and maintaining excitement are lack of support, lack of admiration, and fatigue.

1. Lack of support

Leaders who don't themselves receive consistent encouragement from other sources find it difficult to sustain their own excitement, not to mention anyone else's.

No man is an island. I've lived on islands—in Puerto Rico and the Dominican Republic—for long periods of time. Sometimes I feel like I need to get off the island just to get recharged. The same goes for all of us along our road to cultural mastery. We all need support and encouragement. You can't be a loner if you want to become a cultural leader who can excite others.

Since encouragement is the root of excitement, I must ask you: Who is encouraging *you*? What is the source of *your* excitement? Who is modeling encouragement for you so you can pass it on? If you, like many leaders, find yourself feeling lonely and isolated, you may need to seek out someone in your life who can encourage you on your own path to greatness.

One such person for me is Duane Cummings. Duane is an author, speaker, and highly respected servant leader. Duane not only wrote the foreword to this book, he has been a great source of encouragement to me personally.

A few years ago, when Duane first heard me speak about cultural mastery, he said, "Hey, Ricardo, you need to get this out to the world. People really need to hear this message, and no one is saying it like you do. You should be speaking to thousands of people at a time in major events." Now, *that* was encouraging, to say the least! Then, over a period of several years, Duane continued to talk with me about how important my message and mission was. When I resisted he would just keep encouraging me. He challenged me to expand beyond my niche market of Latino and non-Latino organizational relationships into the broader field of cultural leadership.

Honestly, if it were not for Duane's encouragement, you would not be reading this book. I wouldn't be writing to encourage *you* to become a true cultural master, so you can expand your influence and impact in this culturally complex world. I would still be in my own comfort zone, and the Six Stages of Cultural Mastery would get only a quick mention in a speech or in a few of my courses at Bilingual America. If this book helps you, you may want to thank Duane as well.

> *We cannot excite others if we are not excited about our own life, purpose, and mission.*

Almost always, when someone accomplishes something exciting or impactful in their lives, it is because there was an encourager standing behind them who really lit that fire of excitement.

Do you have a true encourager in your life? If not, find one, pray for one, or at the very least, hire one.

2. Lack of admiration

The second barrier to creating sustained excitement is a lack of honest admiration for the people we lead. It's really difficult to encourage and excite people we don't respect, appreciate, or admire. It can also be difficult to admire people who are very different from us if we don't first understand their cultural framework, nuances, and motivations. Perhaps you can see why Excitement is Stage Four, and not an earlier stage. There is simply no way to maintain excitement about people we do not deeply understand, with whom we have not engaged meaningfully, or for whom we have no true empathy.

To admire means to have a feeling of regard, wonder, pleasure, or approval. Do you have a sense of wonder at the talent or abilities of people who are different from you? Do you draw pleasure from being around people who have different talents than yours? Do you fully appreciate people who are different from you?

> *There is simply no way to maintain excitement about people we do not deeply understand, with whom we have not engaged meaningfully, or for whom we have no true empathy.*

When we don't admire someone, we normally don't value much of what they say. One barometer of inclusive leadership is how often people come to us to share their honest thoughts regarding our vision. Do the people around you have this freedom? If they do not, perhaps you need to pay a bit more attention to why this is the case. We'll normally find the answer right here in Stage Four.

Admiration doesn't mean we necessarily admire *everything* about the people around us, but it does mean we seek out specific things we can admire and proactively focus on.

To admire someone is much different from just accepting or tolerating them. To tolerate people is simply to put up with them—and that is why we should do away with the cultural tolerance mantra. Admiration is a more useful goal than tolerance, and it helps lead us to an even better goal, which you'll get to in Stage Six.

If you accept those under your leadership, that is a great start, but it's a rather *passive* or neutral view of them. Certainly acceptance is a better behavior than rejection, but it isn't enough to create sustained excitement. If I truly admire you, or admire something about you, I am vested in you and your success. Then, and only then, can I get excited enough about you to invest in your potential as a person.

You might start by listening to yourself when you talk about your people. We've all heard leaders say things like, "That person is good for nothing," or "He'll never make it," or "I have no idea how to get her to change her attitude." Do you sound like that? When I hear comments like that, I typically look at the speaker and ask, as politely as possible, "Did you hire the wrong person or do you need to work on how you develop and encourage people?"

Truly admiring those you lead is not just a conduit to your excitement about them; people absolutely need to feel admiration from their leaders to get excited about the organization, the mission, and its leadership. Excitement goes both ways. When you,

> *Truly admiring those you lead is not just a conduit to your excitement about them; people absolutely need to feel admiration from their leaders to get excited about the organization, the mission, and its leadership.*

as the leader, are authentically excited about your people, they will reciprocate by becoming excited about you and your mission.

3. Fatigue

In physics, energy equals work. If you really want to accomplish a lot, you must have high energy. But many leaders are just plain tired, and weariness kills excitement. When roles or responsibilities wear on us day after day and we don't recharge our batteries through proper diet, exercise, spiritual rejuvenation, mental stimulation, and meaningful rest, we won't be very exciting to be around. And we certainly will have little ability to encourage and excite others.

Three Ways to Generate Excitement

What are some practical steps you can take to become a leader who can truly get excited about others so that others can get excited about you? Here are three: attending to your own self-care, finding specific things to admire in others, and clearly defining your organizational mission.

1. **Take care of yourself**. We touched on this earlier: If we want to be encouraging leaders who create excitement, we absolutely must have support and encouragement from others. We must make a commitment to, and be responsible for, taking care of ourselves physically, mentally, emotionally, and spiritually.

   If we're too busy for regular exercise, then we're too busy. If we don't have the discipline to maintain a healthy diet, how can we be healthy enough to encourage and excite people? If we're weighed down with responsibilities and cares, how are we going to lift up and inspire others effectively?

   Here's a hard truth: It is often difficult for people to respond to leaders who are out of shape. For example, public speakers who are in good physical shape are admired more highly than those who are not. Being out of shape makes us lethargic and slow; according to some studies, it also slows down our mental faculties. At the very least, this will be the perception many people will have. And you've heard it before: Perception is reality.

Speak to great leaders who have been leading for a long time, and you'll find that they have learned to recharge by getting away from the pressures of the day-to-day. Some lean into exercise as a getaway; some lean into friends, family, or mentors. Others find rejuvenation in the great outdoors. Whether your place of renewal is in the mountains, by the sea, or perhaps even in the city, get there. As I write this at this moment, I am looking at the ocean on the south coast of the Dominican Republic. I have a home on the north coast, but I found this place to get away, be alone, and study and write. If we want to accomplish great things and provide encouragement and excitement to others, we must take care of ourselves.

2. **Find the best in others**. Even if those you lead have obvious flaws (as we all do), find something that you can admire in them. Every human being has intrinsic worth, and one of our most important jobs as leaders is to find that value, then highlight it and develop it.

Allow me to hold up a different lens so that you can see what I mean when I say we can always find something positive about people, no matter who they are or what they've done. Let's say you have a tough time admiring undocumented immigrants on a personal level.[12] For whatever reason, you're having trouble finding something to admire about people who have entered the country in an illegal manner.

Then let's say the tables are suddenly turned.

Let's say that the United States undergoes a severe and sudden crisis. Corruption, misuse of public monies, and poverty are rampant. Jobs become scarce and you are struggling mightily to support your family. Further, let's say that sometimes your children go hungry and your family is forced to live in a home that is substandard and even dangerous. Maybe, in a worst-case scenario, your family is receiving death threats because you refuse to cooperate with local corrupt officials who want kickbacks.

Now, in this scenario, let's say that just over the border, Mexico is suddenly very prosperous and jobs are plentiful. You find out that you could go to Mexico and get one of those jobs, and your family would be able to eat well and live in safe housing. Would you cross the Mexican border to create a safer, healthier life for your family?

Let's say further that those caught crossing illegally into Mexico are sent back to the United States or detained in Mexico under terrible conditions. And let's say the journey itself is dangerous and expensive. But things at home are so

---

12 The fact that I say "undocumented" may not be agreeable to some people. Some people prefer the term "illegal immigrant." Here's the thing: I don't believe any of God's creations can be illegal. My view on this is not political in nature, it is driven by my view of the intrinsic worth of humanity and my belief that we are all creatures of God. I can't bring myself to call another human being illegal. I can call a person's *actions* illegal based on the laws of a particular country, but I won't call the person illegal.

bad that you and your family decide to take the risk. What does it take for you to make that decision, to risk the journey? Determination? Courage? Faith? Perseverance? Love of family? Could you admire those qualities in someone else?

When I ask these questions at conferences where the audience is filled with people who are adamantly against illegal immigration into the United States, I find that they just go into a blank stare at first, thinking. Then they nod their heads. Yes, they would cross *their* border and yes, they could find something to admire in such a person. This scenario completely changes their view of undocumented immigrants! My point here is not political—it is about learning to admire people we may view as misfits, outcasts, or even worthless. No one is worthless—everyone has value! It is our job as leaders to find this value and develop it.

3. **Clearly define your organizational vision**. "Where there is no vision, the people perish," reads the Book of Proverbs. If you have no unifying vision with the multicultural people you lead, there will be no progress.

Another translation of this Proverb reads, "Where there is no vision, people cast off restraint." In other words, they rebel. People rebel when they feel no connection to their leaders, when they haven't been encouraged to understand and internalize the vision of the organization and when they have had little or no participation in its development.

Why is there so much rebellion from different cultural subsets in the United States? Because there is no compelling or unifying vision that has been set by national leadership.

If we are to excite people of other cultures in our organizations, we must develop a compelling, encouraging, and unifying vision. We must also make sure that our people have a part in the development of the vision so that it is not seen as a top-down

> *Why is there so much rebellion from different cultural subsets in the United States? Because there is no compelling or unifying vision that has been set by national leadership.*

dictatorial mandate. Many people who have lived under corrupt governments or leaders are very sensitive to, and will rebel against, leaders who take a top-down approach. Remember, this is the very reason many people fled their home countries to migrate to the United States or another country in the first place.

As you're developing your vision, it might help to think about cultural differences in terms of what experts call "high-context" and "low-context" cultures. High-context cultures are very relationship-driven. People in high-context cultures find their primary sense of identity through the extended group or family. For example, the Latino culture and many minority cultures are high-context. Low-context cultures, such as mainstream U.S. business culture, are process and results–driven. People in low-context cultures tend to find their primary sense of identity through individual achievement and recognition. People in high-context cultures value tradition over change, while people in low-context cultures value change over tradition.

This is important when you are attempting to change things with people whose culture has a different context level than your own. Go slowly and be highly transparent with people, or you'll likely face resistance, and even questioning of your motives.

When low-context, process and results–driven leaders attempt to lead people from high-context cultures, icebergs collide. There is a real disconnect. These leaders are all about getting things done, but their people need a deeper sense of feeling, admiration, and engagement. Simply put, they need more human connection. Think about this distinction as you work to clarify and communicate your common vision.

The Benefits of Excitement

The fact that you are this far into this book is exciting to me. It says a whole lot more about you and your desire to grow than it does about my writing skills! You are the one seeking knowledge, you are the one seeking understanding, you are the one who wants to excite and inspire a group of people. You have greatness within you and that excites me—it should excite you, too!

At the root of all excitement is encouragement. Are you an encourager? Are you a person who sees the very best in others and helps them to build on those virtues? If so, not only will you be excited about those under your care and influence, but as a byproduct, they will be excited about you and your mission as well.

If you are as excited about the possibilities and potential

> *No one is worthless—everyone has value! It is our job as leaders to find this value and develop it.*

of the people under your influence as I am about you, then you are ready to move into Stage Five of Cultural Mastery.

Resources

- **Fostering admiration for people:** Check out the book *Collaborative Intelligence: Thinking with People Who Think Differently*, by Dawna Markova and Angie McArthur (Spiegel & Grau, 2015). It will help you work with people who think differently from you, either because they're wired that way or because of cultural differences.

- **Servant leadership:** The Greenleaf Center for Servant Leadership, founded by Robert K. Greenleaf is an international nonprofit organization whose mission is "to advance the awareness, understanding, and practice of servant leadership by individuals and organizations." Learn more at greenleaf.org

- **Leadercast:** Leadercast exists to help people become leaders worth following. It offers significant teaching and training through its LeadercastNow online platform, as well as LeadercastLive and LeadercastLabs. Learn more about Leadercast here: leadercast.com

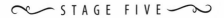 STAGE FIVE

Empowerment

As we look ahead into the next century,
leaders will be those who empower others.

—BILL GATES

P RESIDENT JOHN F. KENNEDY began his term in office in the most uplifting manner. He and his wife, Jacqueline, brought the dawning of a new age to Americans, perhaps to the world: an age of hope and empowerment. Kennedy's inaugural speech underscored his theme of empowering the nation, as he implored Americans, "Do not ask what your country can do for you, ask what you can do for your country." JFK's inaugural words were highly empowering. He was resetting the mentality of the country. He was saying to people: This is about what *you* can accomplish together, not what the government can accomplish for you.

This can-do atmosphere was so powerful it launched the United States into space! At the time, the Soviet Union had successfully launched a cosmonaut into orbit and was conceivably many years ahead of the United States in the race to space. But the Kennedy Administration put resources behind the president's inspiring words, empowering the nation to put a man on the moon by the end of the decade.

Of course, empowerment does not come without risks, as JFK's death so tragically shows. I was three years old when the beloved president was assassinated. It was such an earth-shaking moment that I remember to this day watching as Walter Cronkite described the horrible scene on the black-and-white television set owned by a family we were visiting. Later, during the funeral procession, the image of little John

John saluting his father in that brave stance was embedded on the American psyche.

Empowerment Is a Total Investment

The Kennedy legacy lives on throughout the world. Closer to home, I would like to introduce you to an empowering figure in my own life, Dallas Rohrer. Dallas has been a godsend in my life and empowered me to grow Bilingual America.

I met Dallas after teaching a workshop. He came up to me and said, "Ricardo, you are an excellent teacher but you don't really know how to run this business." This was back in 1992 when I first started the company. I didn't know much about Dallas at the time and I honestly wasn't prepared for his well-meaning directness. As I would soon learn, he was a wealthy Atlanta businessman, with an MBA in Economics from the University of Chicago and an undergraduate degree from the University of Notre Dame. He had attended the workshop with a group of people from his company to learn about Latino culture and also to develop some Spanish language proficiency for his staff.

Initially, when Dallas told me I didn't know how to run the business, I thought he was being rude and I kind of brushed off what he said. He was definitely a low-context person speaking to a high-context Latino! But through that night and the next day his words haunted me. After some self-reflection, I realized he was right. I had a very strong teaching and communications background, but I had never learned how to run and grow a business. So, I picked up the phone and called him. Here's how that conversation went:

Me: "Dallas, do you remember what you said to me the other day? That I don't know how to run the business? Do you really believe that?"

Dallas: "Ricardo, it's just the way it is. Nothing personal. You really don't know how to run your business. That's obvious."

Me: "Would you help me?"

Dallas: "I was just waiting for you to ask. You have such amazing potential for good."

Here's this very successful American business owner willing to mentor this Puerto Rican hillbilly trainer who has a dream to teach people how to maximize their relationships regardless of their backgrounds. He didn't just say, "Hey, Ricardo, you have great potential. I hope the best for you." No, he invested himself in me.

Dallas and I met for lunch nearly every month—for about eight years! And every year for those eight years my company doubled in size. Dallas did not give me money or tangible resources—he gave me much more: He empowered me with knowledge, wisdom, and contacts. He even paid for the lunches! Even after I was doing well financially, he wouldn't let me pay. Over those eight years he learned about me, engaged with me, was empathetic toward me, was excited about me, and empowered me. (By the way, Dallas and I got to Stage Six, which you'll learn in the next chapter, together.)

I want to encourage you: There are other leaders out there who really want to help people like you who have great potential for good. If you don't presently have the resources to empower those you lead, pray for and seek out someone like Dallas who can empower *you*. And make sure that when you do find someone and accomplish your goals, you pay it forward and support others.

Thank you, Dallas! Without you, I would most likely still have a struggling little language and cultural training school on the north side of Atlanta, or maybe I would have become stuck and moved on to something else. You empowered me, and I am forever indebted to you.

What Is Empowerment?

To empower means to put power into people (em-power), so that they can accomplish something of importance to all concerned. Good leadership empowers by inspiring and providing the resources for success. Let's look at how it works.

Articles on empowerment abound in today's business and organizational literature. Many speak of empowerment as creating higher levels of personal autonomy and self-determination. And they miss the point completely: Empowerment is not about creating autonomy or self-determination—it is about providing the resources necessary to allow those under our leadership and influence to join us in fulfilling a vision and mission together.

In Spanish, the noun for "power" is *poder*. It is also a verb: The verb *poder* is translated as "to be able to." In other words, when we truly empower people, we put them in a position *to be able to* accomplish something meaningful for the common good. We provide them with the tools they need to succeed.

Empowerment is active. It is not merely encouraging people to be the best they can be. It's not just about getting people excited about what they might do. It is about providing the necessary resources to allow people to be *able* to excel at whatever it is we determine to accomplish together.

When we tell someone, "*Sí se puede*," ("Yes, you can"), without out also providing them with the tools to do so, we are not empowering. We may be encouraging, but true empowerment goes further: It demonstrates the behaviors needed to achieve, and it provides the tools and support to enable that achievement.

Empowerment is active. It is not merely encouraging people to be the best they can be. It's not just about getting people excited about what they might do. It is about providing the necessary resources to allow people to be able to excel at whatever it is we want to accomplish together.

Three Barriers to Empowerment

As with the other Six Stages of Cultural Mastery, there are barriers to our development of empowerment. As with any of the stages, the biggest barrier to successfully completing this stage is not fully processing the previous stage.

Please consider the three main challenges that leaders face as they seek to become more empowering in their leadership: an unwillingness to share resources, a lack of trust in their people, and a lack of faith in humanity.

1. Unwillingness to share resources

We can encourage people, motivate people, and tell them how great we believe they are, but if we don't provide them with the resources they need to succeed we simply can't be empowering. The reality is that some people talk a good game, but great cultural leaders go beyond providing the venue and also provide the bats, helmets, and balls to play in the game.

Sometimes success requires tangible resources—think of them as power tools that actually empower! This could mean a new computer, an ergonomic desk, software that makes the work more efficient, better hotels for salespeople on the road, and more staff or volunteers. And in addition to these types of tools, it can also mean better salaries or compensation.

> We can't ask people to accomplish a goal for which they simply don't have the resources.

Often the empowering tools are intangible resources, such as training in a new language or skill, connecting to other people, providing time off to recharge, and developing personal career plans, to name a few examples.

The point is, we can't ask people to accomplish a goal for which they simply don't have the resources.

You might be asking, "Why on earth wouldn't I make sure my people have the resources they need?" Well, it depends. To get to the meat of the issue, a better question might be: "Do I know my people well enough to know what resources they need?" If you don't know your people, if you haven't engaged with them, if you don't care deeply for them, truly appreciate their histories, abilities, and promise, and have created a common vision together, then you can't be sure you know what they need. Again, Stage Five requires us to go back and look at how well we've processed the first four stages.

There are other reasons we might be tempted to withhold resources. Sometimes we are not generous with the people we lead because we are insecure and simply don't want to share our knowledge or contacts with others who would benefit. We carefully guard what we feel gives us power or wealth, instead of sharing what could empower the people under our care and influence. Or although we may have the financial resources to empower people, our current focus might be more on present profits than on long-term growth and sustainability.

This reminds me of the joke about a CFO and a CEO. The CFO says to the CEO, "What if we spend all this money to train these people and then they leave?" The CEO answers, "What if we don't and they stay?" (To be fair, I know a lot of very empowering CFOs who would never say that, but you get the point.)

If you have the resources to empower your people, do so. If it blesses them, it will bless you. Unless we provide the necessary resources, it will be impossible to truly empower people. If you have the resources to empower them but don't, this may indicate that you don't really believe in them, or in the vision you have created together.

You may ask what you should do if you don't have the financial or leadership resources necessary to provide for those you want to empower. What if you are a new leader who is not well connected or who has limited financial assets? In that case, your number one job is to find another leader or mentor who will empower *you*.

2. Lack of Trust in Your People
Some leaders just don't trust their people to do what they say they are going to do. Some leaders don't trust in the

abilities of the people on their team. Some leaders are insecure and think that people will take their empowerment and use it against them.

But if we don't trust the people we are called upon to educate and elevate to respond to our leadership, it really says more about us as leaders than it does about them as followers. And our lack of trust will impede our ability to empower.

Of course, we are all human, and our trust in people can be damaged—by betrayal, rejections, disloyalty, and disappointment. But it's important to note that even if you were burned one time, or perhaps several times, your job as a cultural master is still to empower others. When we empower others there is always a risk that they will not respond the way we intend. This gives us the opportunity to practice patience, to try again, to loosen just a little bit our grip on expected outcomes, to trust that eventually our efforts together will bear fruit.

Dallas took a leap when he reached out to me. He had no way to know whether I would respond to his desire to empower me. Conversely, I had no idea how valuable his input and time would be. We both took a risk, but his was greater. All great leaders must be willing to take this risk, to appreciate that our people are also taking a risk with us, and to trust that together we can succeed.

Years after I met Dallas, I thanked him publicly during a speech to the Georgia Association of Latino Elected Officials. He received a standing ovation. Afterward he and I went out to lunch (and no, he still wouldn't let me pay!)

and I said to him, "Dallas, I have no idea how to repay you for all you've done for me." He looked at me straight in the eyes and said, "Ricardo, you have thanked me so many times. Look at what you've accomplished. I'm part of that."

Sometimes, leaders must be bold enough to take the risk and trust other people. You'll be amazed at what true empowerment can, and will, accomplish.

3. Lack of faith in humanity

Sometimes the problem is deeper: We just don't believe in people in general. Our fundamental view of life is negative. We feel jaded, cynical, and pessimistic. Perhaps we feel that we've caught the wrong edge of life far too many times. If this describes you right now, I'm sorry for your suffering.

I also sincerely understand. I know how despair feels.

My mother, Phyllis, was orphaned as a child[13] and suffered major bouts of depression throughout her life. One day, when I was in the fifth grade, I came home from school and found I was the only one of my three siblings in the house. I called out for my mom, who was usually home at this time. There was no answer. I looked in the laundry room, the kitchen, everywhere—but she wasn't there. I walked up the stairs, calling, "Mom, you home?" No answer. I walked into my parents' bedroom to see my mother lying on her bed, her eyes rolled up into her head. I thought she

---

13 My mother was adopted by a wealthy family from Nicholasville, Kentucky. When her adoptive father died, she was not named in his last will and testament, which affected her greatly from an emotional standpoint. In early adulthood she was reunited with her biological mother. This is the grandmother I mentioned in the Preface, saying, "Now, Ricky, now stop that, Ricky!" To me, she was always Granny.

was dead. I had the presence of mind to call 911 and the paramedics came. I'll never forget them strapping her to a straightjacket and taking her down that flight of stairs. She had attempted suicide with an overdose of pills.

This was one of the most horrifying moments of my life. It deeply shook my faith in life and in humanity at a very young age. I'm sure now that this is why I studied theology and psychology: most likely I was seeking answers for what would become a life-long journey of recovery.

If you, too, have been shaken to the core of your soul, and in some way have lost faith in humanity, I encourage you to take your pain and make it your gain. Remember Dr. Wayne Dyer's story? Get his book and read the whole thing—let it sink into your soul. Seek out the help you need so that you can fully believe that we choose how we are going to respond to life's difficulties and challenges.

For us to become Cultural Masters, we must have faith in people—not just people like us, but people from all cultures. We must believe in their intrinsic good and their ability to achieve great and wonderful things for themselves, their families, their communities, and their world. You, as a cultural leader, are an important part of this cycle of humanity.

Life won't stop throwing us curve balls that hit us straight in the head. But neither will it stop surprising us with delight and wonder. Here's one small example: Dallas and I had something huge in common that I didn't learn until later in our friendship: We'd practically spent our high school years in the same zip code! I went to Concord High School in Elkhart, Indiana, while about 15 years earlier

Dallas had gone to Concord's rival, Jimtown High School. What's more, he was from the Rohrer family, who owned Rohrer's Heating and Air Conditioning just down the road from El Toro, my parents' Mexican restaurant.

Life really is an amazing adventure. This gives me faith. I hope it inspires you, as well, to believe in the greatness of our world and not to get stuck in the mud of disbelief.

Three Ways to Empower Others

Now that I've shared the main barriers to our empowerment of other people, what steps can you take to empower others? Here are some suggestions I hope you'll find helpful.

1. Assess individual talent

We cannot develop talent that we don't know exists. Before embracing this empowerment movement with those you lead, make sure you fully understand their talents, desires, and motivators. I'm referring to your assessment of their individual abilities and their talents, not your general knowledge of their culture. The purpose of this type of individual assessment is to get a clear understanding of how the person can best be empowered by leveraging their strengths and helping them correct any limiting weaknesses.

There are many helpful talent and personality assessment tools on the market today. The main qualities you want to know about the people you lead are listed below.

A. Identify their specific area of intelligence. You can start with the VARK Questionnaire I mentioned in the previous chapter. To delve deeper, though, I would recommend Dr. Howard Gardner's outstanding work on the seven types of intelligence. Some people have linguistic intelligence, while others have logical intelligence. Some people have musical intelligence, while others have mechanical intelligence. People view life and approach projects from different perspectives, and they come from different talent pools. As a cultural leader, it is your job to know your people.

By the way, always remember that level of education doesn't necessarily equate with level of intelligence. My father, Pablo, had an eighth-grade education and spoke no English when he arrived in the United States. But he was highly intelligent and became a very successful businessman, able to retire when he was only 45. As they say, "Only in America." It's entirely possible that you may have the opportunity to lead people who, if given the chance and put on the right track, could achieve great levels of success and influence, even though they don't have the highest level of formal education.

As mentioned previously, we can't lead people to the highest levels until we know them at the deepest levels. The assessment process is critical to getting to know them personally at the deeper levels.

B. Identify personal motivators. What drives your people personally? What will motivate them to share your mission? Leaders who are Cultural Masters are part-time psychologists—they are always seeking to understand what will motivate people to action. You can then structure your message so you can dialogue with a person or group to meet their specific personal motivators. Note: You must be sincere in your efforts to understand and empower, or people will see through you very quickly, especially people of other cultures who are already highly sensitized to hypocrisy and corruption.

C. Identify professional motivators. Although it is perhaps not ideal, many people tend to separate their personal goals and motivators from their professional ones. Wise leaders who seek to empower others must have a clear understanding of the career or vocational goals of the people they lead, as well as of what drives them personally. It is next to impossible to keep someone motivated toward a mission or goal if they don't understand what's in it for them and how it benefits the overall organization. It is our job to clearly understand, without judgment, the professional goals of our people. One word of caution here: If there is a person under your care who is capable of doing a job you really want done but it is *not in their line of passion*, don't give them that job just to fill the need. Cultural leaders respect the psychological needs of the people under their care and don't place people into unwanted positions, emotionally or motivationally, just because they are good at something. Eventually, those people will leave, or else disengage and simply lose all passion for the leader and the organization.

2. Allocate resources wisely

When you empower people, you must provide them with the resources they need to be able to do what you ask of them. The challenge is, our resources are limited. So empowering people requires wise resource allocation.

Resource allocation requires planning. People only have so much bandwidth; the same is true for organizations. You may find that you need to go outside your organization to find needed resources, maybe from a training institute, or even perhaps from outside investors. Those are leadership decisions you must make. The key here is working with your team members and stakeholders to identify the highest priorities. Wise resource allocation means helping them understand, and appreciate, the resources you *do* bring to the table, as well as whatever limitations in resources you may have.

By the time we reach Stage Five, our people should trust our decisions about resources. No one under our influence should be concerned about our intent. They should know our heart. They should know we're all-in for them.

As my friend Duane Cummings said in a Leadercast-NOW video interview, "Trust is backed up by intent. If you've ever wondered, Should I trust that person? or if right off the bat you have a weird instinct like, Oh, I don't know if I trust them, that's because you're concerned about their intent."[14] By this stage of cultural mastery, we're all-in for our people and team. There should be no question about our intent at this point.

And we only get so much relational capital from our associates or partners. In other words, we can't draw from the same well too many times or it will go dry on us. Just as we only have limited bandwidth, so too do our associates and partners. So wise empowerment leaders learn to allocate these resources for maximum impact based on mission and

---

14 Duane Cummings, "How Do You Define Ethical Leadership?" Leadercast-NOW website, leadercast.com/programs/how-do-you-define-ethical-leadership.

human priority. You can't provide everything to everyone at all times, and the people you lead shouldn't expect everything of you. But if you know them, engage with them, have empathy for them, are excited about them, and empower them, chances are they will trust that you will allocate resources in a way that best supports the organization, and you will make their needs a priority to the degree that you can. This is how they will trust you and your heart's intent.

So if you consistently have people questioning you and your leadership, if you experience more turnover than you should, and if people feel they are not heard—then you have an issue of trust. People are resisting you because they don't truly know your intent. If you are experiencing this, it might help to look at the Six Stages and see where you should focus your attention.

3. Hold people accountable

Dallas taught me so much over the years—from practical business processes to truths about human nature. I am sure that if I hadn't applied what he was teaching me, he eventually would have decided that he had better things to do with his time.

Results matter, and being a cultural master doesn't mean you ignore unmet goals or poorly performed tasks just because you don't want to offend a person of another culture. All people need to be held accountable for how they invest and leverage the resources provided to them. Not to hold people accountable for fear of offending them does a disservice to both the organization and the people we are leading.

To hold the people we lead accountable, we may need to understand how they are held accountable within their cultures. It makes sense, doesn't it? Think about children—in some cultures, telling them that you're going to tell their mother about something they did wrong is a lot more meaningful than saying you're going to tell their father. (And in other cultures, it's vice versa.) It's similar for grownups: In some cultures, calling someone out in public works; in others, it's important to allow people to save face.

> *To hold the people we lead accountable, we may need to understand how they are held accountable within their cultures.*

Part of being a cultural master is learning to structure accountability programs and approaches in ways that work without being offensive or unnecessarily touching deep levels of personal or community sensitivity. In other words, if you say and do the same thing with all people, you'll never get the same results. This touches on the mistaken mantra of *fairness* that many American managers espouse.

> *Some people believe that fairness, or equality, means leaders should treat everyone the same. This is neither wise nor effective when you are working with people of different cultures.*

Some people believe that fairness, or equality, means leaders should treat everyone the same. This is neither wise nor effective when you are working with people of different cultures. Yes, you should be *just* with everyone, but the same approach does not work with everyone, and it's important to develop this awareness and experience.

Equality doesn't mean justice.

This is equality.   This is justice.

The same is true in business and organizational management. If, in the name of fairness, I treat everyone exactly the same way, I will get very inconsistent results. If you study the picture above, you'll notice that equality would demand that everyone gets one box to stand on. Some leaders have bought into the idea that, to be *fair*, everyone should be treated in the same manner. Wise leaders, however, know that to get consistent results, they need to adjust the number of boxes accordingly. Some people simply need more, or different, resources to produce the same results.

People and processes are unique. While it is true that great businesses have consistent processes that are equally applied, it is also true that the people who are applying those processes on behalf of the organization respond differently to different approaches and modes of communication from their leaders.

If the people you're leading are not responding to your accountability processes, or if people are complaining about lack of fairness, it may be time to assess your evaluation and education process. You may need to educate yourself further on some cultural specifics of accountability. You may also need to educate your associates on the differences between equality and justice. This will allow them to understand and accept your decision-making processes without questioning whether you are being "fair" in your distribution of resources.

> *All people view life differently, and if we try to treat everyone the same—even when it comes to holding them accountable—we will not become Cultural Masters who effectively lead and empower our people.*

All people view life differently, and if we try to treat everyone the same—even when it comes to holding them accountable—we will not become Cultural Masters who effectively lead and empower our people.

The Benefits of Empowerment

When we truly empower those we influence, our work as Cultural Masters and leaders starts to bear fruit in abundance. People who have been empowered take the energy and resources we have invested in them and return it hundredfold: They not only embrace the group's calling, they expand it.

Empowerment takes resources and a very proactive commitment to the common good. We must be committed to putting power into our people. As we have seen, empowering others involves (1) accurately assessing talent and matching people to their skills and passion; (2) ensuring that we allocate resources wisely; and (3) setting clear goals and ensuring that our people agree to the outcomes to which we will hold them accountable in a culturally relevant manner. Remember, if it's not culturally relevant, it's not relevant.

No one gets to true empowerment without processing and mastering the first four Stages. To truly empower our

If it's not culturally relevant, it's not relevant.

people, we'll need to deeply understand their internal motivations and cultural frameworks and have passion for their abilities and potential.

Next, we reach the pinnacle—Stage Six: Endearment. I think you're going to find this the most rewarding stage of all.

Resources

- **On identifying types of intelligence:** Howard Gardner, *Multiple Intelligences: New Horizons in Theory and Practice.* New York: Basic Books, 2006. See also Dr. Gardner's website at howardgardner.com/multiple-intelligences.

- **Accountability:** Consider checking out Alan Dobzinski's S.P.E.E.D accountability program at accountabilityexperts. com. In addition, Sam Silverstein is a recognized expert in the area of accountability as a competitive advantage. You can find out more about Sam at samsilverstein.com.

- **Center for International Development Empowerment Lab at Harvard University:** The Empowerment Lab exists to seek sustainable solutions to poverty and to empower the economically disadvantaged. The center sponsors events, provides research, and offers avenues for engagement. You can learn more about the lab at: hks.harvard.edu/centers/cid/programs/empowerment-lab/

 STAGE SIX

Endearment

To love without knowing how to love
wounds the person we love.

—THICH NHAT HANH

D URING MY CHILDHOOD, MY Puerto Rican father
was not very positive in his views about Mexican people. For his own reasons, he just didn't like them. He did, however, like to play poker. And he liked to win.

When I was around seven years old, my father met a man
everyone called "Mexican Joe." Mexican Joe was a card shark,
and over the next few years he helped my father win thousands
of dollars on the weekends from unsuspecting poker partners.
He was my first real introduction to Mexicans.

I had heard my whole childhood from my Puerto Rican
father that Mexicans are not good people and he didn't want
them around us. Mexican Joe, despite his career choice, was a
jovial and positive guy, and through his friendship, my father
began to change his views about Mexicans. Of course, their
friendship wasn't just about playing cards. My dad, ironically
enough, had a Mexican restaurant, so Mexican Joe was able to
educate him about some of the foods and other cultural nuances. They also engaged together on a few construction projects
at our house.

Then Mexican Joe hit some difficult times. My dad, on the
other hand, had become very successful with his Mexican restaurants. He embodies the American dream and is a constant
light of inspiration for me personally. By the time Mexican
Joe's luck ran out, my dad was doing quite well.

By that time, Joe and my dad had engaged together so often that my dad had developed empathy for him as well. He didn't know it, but my father had gone through Stages One, Two, and Three on a personal level. This is another thing about the Six Stages: They work as well in our personal relationships as they do in corporate, organizational, or community relationships. They can have a huge impact on the health of our families and with our closest friends.

My dad's empathy for Mexican Joe during this time took him to Stages Four and Five. I remember my dad trying to encourage him to find a better lifestyle. Dad also made the ultimate commitment to extend resources to him so he could be empowered to get his life back together. Mexican Joe actually came to live with us in our home.

My dad was a very traditional *macho* Latino male back in those days, but he had a special relationship with Mexican Joe. He loved him. He was willing to sacrifice for him. Although I had no conception of it then, my dad's relationship with Mexican Joe took me vicariously through all six stages of cultural mastery.

There's another, better-known story that's reflective of the Six Stages of Cultural Mastery. Two young men from entirely different cultures and social strata became friends. David was a lowly ranch hand, and Jonathan was the son of a wealthy and powerful king. Neither of them could truly understand the other's world. There was absolutely no good reason for them to work together for the common good of their country. In time, however, they moved through all six stages of cultural mastery. They came to love each other.

Jonathan's father, the king, hated David and did everything in his power to have the young ranch hand marginalized, even killed. But Jonathan did everything he could to save David's life, even in defiance of his father. As the story relates, "The soul of Jonathan was knit to the soul of David, and Jonathan loved him as his own soul."[15]

As you may recognize, this is the biblical story of Jonathan and David, and it reflects the Six Stages of Cultural Mastery. These two young men had absolutely no reason to be endeared to each other—they were from completely different backgrounds and social classes.

My father's relationship with Mexican Joe and Jonathan's relationship with David both embody endearment, the crescendo of the Six Stages: In Stage Six, we actually love one another—we do not merely tolerate one another, or accept one another. We do not merely work together—we *love* one another. This is how true Cultural Masters create connection: They sincerely love the people they lead, and those people love their leaders. If we get to Stage Six and we love other people and cultures but they don't love us back, then we're not in Stage Six together. We're alone in our love, and we need to step back to a previous stage to get here together.

Do you remember Thomas Sproul, the gentleman who opposed my appearance at his association meeting, and who a couple years later came to promote my speech? I'll never forget his words about Hispanics: "I learned to love these people." That's the ultimate and greatest goal: love.

---

15 1 Samuel 18:1.

The core principle of love is the willingness to sacrifice for one another. This should be the basis of all collaboration. In the best collaboration efforts, ego is put aside and all parties are committed to sacrificing together for the common good.

What Is Endearment?

It is common to start a letter in English by saying, "Dear [name]." We may not think of it every time we write it, but the word *dear* means "something or someone you hold close to your heart." *Endearment* means to hold someone or something within your heart and soul. In Spanish, the word for "endearment" is *cariño*. It's the soft side of love. It's love, which is more than a feeling—it's a willingness to sacrifice oneself. The Sixth Stage of Culture Mastery—Endearment—is a stage of the heart. It is the authentic result that grows out of the previous five stages.

> The goal of intercultural relations should not be tolerance, acceptance, or even agreement. It should be endearment.

When we experience true endearment there is mutual love. It is not one-sided. We may be able to say we love other people, but do they love us back? If not, as previously mentioned, we haven't arrived at Stage Six together.

> When the people under our care are truly endeared to us, not only do we hold them dear to our hearts, but they also hold us close to their hearts.

When the people under our care are truly endeared to us, not only do we hold them dear to our hearts, but they also hold us close to their hearts. Do the people you lead hold you close to their hearts? Are they willing to make extraordinary sacrifices for you as their leader? Would your followers, or the people with whom you work, make personal sacrifices for the good of the overall mission by which you are bound? Some people call this loyalty. It is, in fact, endearment—much deeper than loyalty.

Three Barriers to Endearment

Let's face it—it's not easy to love. We don't often see cultural leaders who love and are truly loved by the people they lead. That's because there are some very distinct barriers to endearment, and it's important to consider them in order to get to this beautiful stage. There are three obstacles for leaders to overcome to get to endearment: the limits of tolerance and agreement, the pain of love, and pride.

1. The limits of tolerance and agreement

As mentioned, many of us have bought into the idea that tolerance is enough in regard to people outside our own group. It is not. Tolerance is better than hate, but love, not tolerance, is the antithesis to hate.

Tolerance is better than hate, but love, not tolerance, is the antithesis to hate.

To tolerate someone means to put up with them. If we're just putting up with each other, there is no way we will achieve great things together.

Again, the goal of intercultural relations should not be tolerance, acceptance, or even agreement. It should be *endearment*. We will never heal our countries, our communities, or our companies until we get serious about going through all Six Stages of Cultural Mastery and arrive at endearment.

I don't want to simply tolerate you. I don't want to simply accept you. I want to love you.

I want atheists and agnostics to love Christians, and Christians (as they are commanded) to love atheists and agnostics.

I want Latinos to love non-Latinos, and non-Latinos to love Latinos.

I want white people to love black people, and black people to love white people.

I want LGBTQ+ people to love heterosexual people, and heterosexual people to love LGBTQ+ people.

I want Muslims to love Westerners and Westerners to love Muslims.

One of the reasons that people cannot love is fear. There is no fear in love—perfect love drives out fear.[16] The only way to fully conquer our fears of other cultures and ways of life is through love.

Tolerance and acceptance are worthy goals but they should not be our end goal. They cannot be our end goal, since neither can overcome our fear—only love can do so. In addition, consensus, or total agreement—agreeing with one another on everything—is an impossible goal. We are not divided

We are not divided because we disagree, we are divided because we are disagreeable.

because we disagree, we are divided because we are disagreeable. And fighting with one another, or insulting one another,

---

because we don't agree with one another is grade-school bullying. We should eliminate it from the public discourse. It is killing the soul of our people, and thus, our country.

Do we have to agree with one another in order to love one another? Absolutely not! I love my wife but I don't always agree with her, nor does she with me. I love my children but I don't always agree with their decisions, nor do they with mine. Endearment doesn't require agreement.

Frankly, we have the wrong goals.

The thing about endearment is that you can't force it. You can't make it happen through civic activism, political mandate, or corporate policies. You can't policy love into being! It will happen only when we go through the stages of education, engagement, empathy, excitement, and empowerment first. It is an issue of the heart.

2. The pain of love

The rock band Nazareth put it like this:

> *Love hurts*
> *Love scars*
> *Love wounds and marks*
> *Any heart not tough or strong enough*
> *To take a lot of pain, take a lot of pain*
> *Love is like a cloud, it holds a lot of rain*
> *Love hurts*
> *Ooo-oo, love hurts.*

Yes, it's true—love hurts. Sometimes we don't want to love because we don't want to be disappointed or rejected or betrayed. Again, Stage Six is not for the faint of heart—it is for secure and stable leaders who are clear about who they are and why they are put on this culturally complex planet.

The crazy thing is, until our followers see and trust our love for them, it will be nearly impossible for them to love us back. We must lead in love and take the first step. This leadership is the essence of cultural mastery. We don't wait for those who follow us to set the example, or to act in a way that is "worthy" of our love. If we want to be in a position to effect meaningful and lasting change, we must commit ourselves to loving first. It won't happen if we just react or respond to the people we lead. Simply put, we must lead with love if we want others to love us and our mission. We must also lead with love if we want those under our influence to love one another in the organization. To do this despite the pain that comes with love takes courage and faith.

And to be honest, it also takes time, and for some people investing more time in others is painful or comes at a high cost. To illustrate this, I want to share with you something we discussed in one of our Cultural Mastery learning cohorts.

To be as culturally relevant as possible in our approach, we offer Cultural Mastery courses for many different professions: for business leaders, educators, law enforcement leaders, sales professionals, nonprofit leaders, public servants, and more. One of our courses is for ministry leaders.

In one of our learning cohorts for ministry leaders, a clergy participant said the following (and I'm paraphrasing): "Well, this is all fantastic. But honestly, and I'm ashamed to say this, I am just too busy to love like this." I thanked him for his honesty and transparency, and no one else said a word for several long, awkward moments.

Does this pastor's admission resonate with you? All of us have limited bandwidth, and we're all stretched by life. To go through the Six Stages and be mindful of them takes time. It takes physical, emotional, and spiritual energy. It's not always easy.

My response at that moment was "If 'the greatest of these is love,' and we don't have time to love, maybe we're just focusing on the wrong things." We then had a wonderful discussion about how the pain of being stretched can cause us to want to jump straight to Stage Six without putting in the work of Stages One through Five. Unfortunately, it just doesn't happen this way. It is a process, and perhaps it's more linear than we would like to think.

3. Pride

Prideful people can't love others. Love requires humility of heart and spirit. Love means we are willing to sacrifice ourselves for those with whom we work and live. Prideful and arrogant leaders can't do such things. They prod and push others to do their bidding, relying on authority and even domination. Meaningful collaboration happens naturally in an environment of endearment because people who truly love one another will work together for the common good, not their own good. That's the essence of love: to give up our own agenda for the common good.

True servant leaders believe that their calling is to elevate and educate those under their care. One friend says the title of CEO should be renamed from Chief Executive

Officer to Chief Elevating Officer. He's right! Loving leadership is servant leadership. We are not called to push and prod, we are called to educate and elevate.

Three Ways to Nurture Endearment

It seems somewhat incongruous to give you a list of things you can do to be more endeared to other people, and to find others endearing! Most of us consider endearment to be more of an internal, intangible emotion, and it is, to a large degree. But that doesn't mean we can't nurture it.

I mentioned early on that the Six Stages have a balance of three proactive stages (education, engagement, and empowerment) and three emotive stages (empathy, excitement, and endearment). Although endearment is largely an emotive stage, is does drive us to real sacrifice, at which point it moves from the heart to the hand. In other words, when we are truly endeared with others, we'll also be compelled to *do* something for them. We'll be called to sacrifice, we'll be called to give ourselves up for the common good.

> *Although endearment is largely an emotive stage, is does drive us to real sacrifice, at which point it moves from the heart to the hand.*

It's clear, there are no shortcuts around the previous five stages. They are, in fact, necessary to get to true endearment, which doesn't happen in a vacuum. Here are some practical suggestions that may help you to become more endeared with your people: (1) loving in a culturally relevant way, (2) dreaming together, and (3) being thankful.

1. Love in a culturally relevant way

What may look like love to you may or may not resonate with the person or people you are leading.

As Zen Buddhist teacher Thich Nhat Hanh said, "To love without knowing how to love wounds the person we love." Think about that. Not only does loving without knowing how not resonate, it actually wounds. It can actually offend and deepen our divides.

I am convinced that many leaders have very good intentions about improving cultural and race relations. But good intentions have never been enough. Way back in 1105, Saint Bernard of Clairvaux wrote, *"L'enfer est plein de bonnes volontés ou désirs,"* from which we get the colloquial saying, "The road to hell is paved with good intentions." As cultural leaders, we must move from having good, albeit misguided, intentions to loving in culturally relevant and meaningful ways. As I mentioned in the previous stage, if it's not culturally relevant, it's not relevant.

In the ministry group discussion described above, one person said, "Well, we're commanded to tell the truth. We have to confront people with themselves." This reminded me of a Scripture passage that reads "Speak the truth in love."

For years, I had been led to believe that speaking the truth in love means we should speak truth in a loving tone of voice. But I've since learned a completely different interpretation. To me, speaking the truth in love means to speak truth within the context of a loving environment; in other words, we gain the right to speak truth when we are in an endearing relationship.

So, yes, we're commanded to speak the truth. We might think that the way to do this is to challenge people, and to make sure our tone of voice sounds loving. But it's an entirely different matter to *gain the right to speak openly with others.* This happens not by changing our tone of voice or imagining that we are "confronting people with themselves." It happens when we are relating with one another in a full context of love—or, we might say, when we're in Stage Six *together.*

Make it your mission to know your people so deeply (Stage One) that you love them in ways they can feel and understand. Don't assume that, just because you personally respond to a particular display of affection or endearment, they will do so

> *Make it your mission to know your people so deeply that you love them in ways they can feel and understand.*

as well. I can't say it often enough: *We can't lead people to the highest levels until we know them at the deepest levels.*

What does it mean to love with cultural relevance? It means to take into consideration the person's (or group's) heritage, how they view relationships, what they deeply value, their tastes for music, their tastes for food, their language preferences, and much more, including many of the elements we have covered in the previous stages.

This requires me as a leader to step out of my world and into another's. It requires me to ask myself, How will this person best respond to my love? How do I love them in a way that will truly endear them to me and my leadership? Are we truly in Stage Six together? Is there an environment of endearment in which we can speak together? It requires me to be a cultural master.

2. Dream together

Nothing creates a bond like sharing a common vision together. Great cultural leaders are great collaborators. They don't just say to people, "Hey, here's my idea, get on board. My way or the highway." No, they actually create the dream together with the people they are leading. They realize that unless the dream is shared, there will never be a true bond.

Alan Schaefer, collaboration master and founder of Banding People Together, says that a leader's main job is to create the conditions where divergent views can converge. A former bandleader who has worked with Grammy-award-

Love prospers and grows when people share a common dream.

winning producers and hit songwriters, Alan has taught me a lot about collaboration. As a musician, he talks about "optimizing the mix" and "getting everyone playing from the same sheet of music." And he's right—collaboration is very much like making music together. Each member of the band has a unique perspective and thought process that, when amplified, adds to the totality of the sound and ultimately the result. This is what we as leaders do: We create a safe place where people's divergent views and perspectives can be blended into beautiful music. If we don't do this, we'll never achieve our greatest potential together.

One stanza of the song "Let Your Love Flow," by the Bellamy Brothers, goes like this:

Just let your love flow like a mountain stream
And let your love grow with the smallest of dreams
And let your love show and you'll know what I mean
It's the season.

It is, indeed, the season for us as cultural leaders to begin to create dreams together with people who are different from ourselves. This isn't about filling diversity quotas, or being inclusive. You see, cultural diversity requires that everyone *gets* in the game. Cultural inclusion requires that everyone *plays* in the game. *Cultural Mastery ensures that everyone wins in the game.* If we have diversity and inclusion but do not get to true endearment, we will never achieve our full potential together.

Love prospers and grows when people share a common dream. This is one of the reasons America continues to struggle so deeply with racial tensions: Our leaders have not brought the country together to create and share a common dream or vision—they have not gone through themselves, nor led us through, the necessary stages of cultural mastery.

Cultural diversity requires that everyone gets in the game. Cultural inclusion requires that everyone plays in the game. Cultural Mastery ensures that everyone wins in the game.

3. Be thankful

Being grateful is transformative. It is the one thing we can do that will most quickly move us toward endearment and maintain the love that we have fostered together.

When we are truly thankful for the people we lead, it changes us and also allows us to become true encouragers—

which, you now know, creates excitement. What would it mean to the people you work with or lead for them to hear you say, "I'm grateful for you," "I appreciate you"?

Or as my Cuban friend Yovany once said to me, "*I celebrate you.*" Now, *that* was truly meaningful to me. It was as if he was saying, "Hey man, when I think about you it's like a party in my soul." Well, Yovany Jérez, I celebrate you too!

If you are white, are you thankful for African Americans in your community? Do you celebrate them, or do you criticize them?

If you are African American, are you thankful for white people in your community? Do you celebrate them, or do you judge them for the sins of past generations?

If you are Christian, do you celebrate the Muslim people in your community? Are you thankful for them, or are you afraid of them?

If you are Muslim, do you celebrate the Christian people in your organization? Are you thankful for them, or do reject them and their values?

I'll never forget a conversation I had some years back with an African-American chief of police in a major U.S. city.[17] At dinner, after a conference I held for his force, he leaned over to me and asked me if he could ask a question privately. I said of course. Then he shared with me that a lot of Mexicans had moved into his neighborhood and he just didn't know quite how to handle their music and all the cars parked in front of their houses. Honestly, I was a bit

17 Unfortunately, to protect this person and his identity, I cannot share details about the city or jurisdiction.

surprised to meet a black man in America who was having trouble with Mexicans moving in. But it brought home to me that none of us is immune from cultural challenges; we all have something to learn about each other. Then we had a satisfying conversation about celebrating one another and finding ways to collaborate for the common good.

Is this getting a bit uncomfortable? Perhaps. Do you want to be a cultural master? Do you want to do the internal work necessary to be in a position to help change the world for good? If so, you must go through this process. And as I hope you realize by now, it may indeed be uncomfortable at times.

If we don't learn to sincerely love one another, the best we can hope for is to tolerate and put up with one another. In the worst-case scenario, we'll wage war against one another. We will continue to meet in our self-imposed segregated business silos and special-interest groups all over America. We'll never achieve Martin Luther King Jr.'s dream in which everyone is judged by the content of their character rather than by the color of their skin.

It's time we start being deeply thankful for people who are different from us. If we cannot honestly pray, "Thank you for the Black / older / White / civilian / Chinese / Democrat / straight / Jewish / Mexican / young / Muslim / Millennial / immigrant / Southern / Gay / Indian / foreign / German / Christian / gringo / Choctaw / Republican / atheist / and [insert cultural group here] people in my family, my community, my organization, my world," then we cannot graduate from the Six Stages.

Now, let me be clear: I am not talking about accepting or tolerating inhumane or criminal behavior from any cultural group. However, when we get to endearment we can find love in our souls even for those we might otherwise deem different or adversarial. And perhaps in the process, we may find that we can work with, influence, and empower someone who will in turn have a greater impact than we alone would have.

The fastest path to true endearment is gratitude. And the fastest way to destroy love is criticism borne out of a bitter or judgmental heart.

The Benefits of Endearment

As all the songs and religions say, love is the answer. Endearment is the most powerful force in the world.

True endearment isn't easy. This is tough internal work for most of us. We can't force ourselves to love. Endearment is the outgrowth of education, engagement, empathy, excitement, and empowerment.

Every one of us came to our views about people from other cultures through our own culture, the way my dad taught me to dislike Mexicans. I didn't know as a child that having negative views of Mexicans was unhealthy. It was modeled to me and I adopted it without even knowing I was doing it.

This is what happens: many people don't really know how, or when, they got such a negative view of people from other cultures. They heard it, they saw it, they lived it, and now they, and those they project it onto, live with it.

However, every one of us can learn, can grow, can broaden and shape our cultural quotients. We don't do this by putting others down, insulting them, or calling them words like "bigot," "hateful," "deplorable," "xenophobic." It just doesn't work like that.

It's important to note that none of us is exempt from this. If we have been the target of stereotyping and discrimination, we may be tempted to respond in kind. That's why some of us seem to live so much on the defensive. Other than the clear struggle we've faced for equality or justice, we face another real risk: by focusing so much on our fight, on the people we feel are oppressing us, we stop loving. If we focus entirely on those who mistreat us, we run the risk of becoming just as unloving and caustic. Relationships go both ways—both sides must come to the table if we're going to achieve the common good.

Many people don't really know how, or when, they got such a negative view of people from other cultures. They heard it, they saw it, they lived it, and now they, and those they project it onto, live with it.

Endearment fulfills a basic human need. *Everyone* needs respect and love, even those we may disagree with, or those who have hurt us. This is true whether or not you are in the majority. Everyone needs to be artfully and thoughtfully brought to the table to go through this process. This is why what you are doing here is so important.

We desperately need cultural leaders who will model what it means to truly know, appreciate, empower—and truly love—people who are different from themselves. This includes knowing, appreciating, empowering, and loving the Southern person who was raised to dislike nonwhites as much as it includes knowing, appreciating, empowering, and loving a Muslim or Latino family seeking refuge. We all have deep human needs; it is our job as leaders to meet people where they are, care for them, encourage them, empower them, and love them.

We are called to love all people, not just the ones we're comfortable with.

Resources

• **Loving in culturally relevant ways:** Gary Chapman is best known for his excellent book, *The Five Love Languages: The Secret to Love That Lasts*, which focuses on marriage. His principles can be applied to cultural leadership as well—see especially *The Five Languages of Appreciation in the Workplace* (Northfield Publishing, 2012), which he cowrote with Paul White.

• **Cultural and ethnic influences on love and attachment:** Published by the Cambridge University Press in 1994, this interesting report explores different cultural and ethnic influences on love and attachment from a sociological standpoint. I find this to be an intriguing report, and, although it is a bit academic, I recommend it. It will introduce you to the concepts of individualism and collectivism in love and acceptance. Written by University of Hawaii professors R. William Doherty, Elaine Hatfield, Kari Thompson, and Patricia Choo.

- **"Languages of Love:** 10 unusual terms of endearment":
  In this article, Paul Noble, with consultants to Collins
  Dictionary, provide us with 10 global terms of endearment. In which language can you call someone a "lump of
  sugar" or a "gazelle" or a "fruit of my heart" or even "my
  flea?" Find out here: bbc.co.uk/news/magazine-22699938

Your Next Step

Step by step and the thing is done.

—CHARLES ATLAS

I SINCERELY HOPE THAT THIS unveiling of the Six Stages of Cultural Mastery has been both inspiring and challenging to you on a deep personal level, as writing it has been for me. Indeed, the journey to cultural mastery is nothing if not personal. On this journey you

> *A leader who is a cultural master strives to find perfect balance between the hand and the heart.*

develop as a cultural master and leader by applying to your own life and community the very specific steps you've just learned. It is about finding a perfect balance between proactive behaviors and deep emotions. A leader who is a cultural master strives to find perfect balance between the hand and the heart.

You can apply the Six Stages of Cultural Mastery to your family, your company, your organization, your faith community, your neighborhood, and even your country. The truths are timeless and transcendent. They work at all levels of relationships and will work as well today as they will 200 years from now.

Looking forward, I'm excited to tell you that once you've worked through the Six Stages and are reaping the benefits, there is a next step for you to take.

As important as it is to transform oneself, all leaders are also called to help transform the world around them. The next step will require you to become a person who actively creates cultural transformation in your broader world, whether in your family, organization, community, or country. The focus will move from developing your own growth and relationships to the transformation of the broader culture for the common good. You see, once we are Cultural Masters, we are in an outstanding position to lead this much-needed change.

Of course, before you take this next step, I encourage you to fully learn, adopt, internalize, and model the Six Stages of Cultural Mastery, or you simply won't be ready to lead cultural transformation. So stick with the Six Stages until you know you've mastered them—at least with the group on which you are focusing. Keep learning, keep practicing, keep engaging, and have patience with yourself. If you would like to deepen your own understanding and internal transformation, I invite you to consider taking one of our Cultural Mastery courses. It is a very powerful experience. You can see more about them at CulturalMastery.com/Courses.

I look forward to hearing your stories of personal and professional connection and cultural mastery. I have every confidence that together we will see the effects of your learning, adoption and modeling of the Six Stages of Cultural Mastery in the world around us, in great and positive ways.

Ricardo González

Appendix

Answers to Athlete Exercise in Stage One:

Roberto Clemente → Puerto Rico

Memo Ochoa → Mexico

Leonel Messi → Argentina (Moved to Spain when young)

Fernando Valenzuela → Mexico

Greg Louganis → United States—LGBTQ+

Rory McElroy → Northern Ireland

Steffi Graff → Germany

Billy Jean King → United States—LGBTQ+

Cristiano Ronaldo → Portugal

Miguel Cabrera → Venezuela

Yao Ming → China

BECOME A CERTIFIED
CULTURAL MASTER

Expand your Influence. Protect your Brand.

FIND OUT MORE:
https://culturalmastery.com/courses

Courses available for:
Business Leaders • Educators
Health Care Professionals
Law Enforcement • Ministry Leaders
Public Servants • Nonprofit Leaders
Sales Professionals • Sport Executives

(customized courses available for qualifying organizations)